CHRISTIAN HEROES: THEN & NOW

DIETRICH BONHOEFFER

In the Midst of Wickedness

CHRISTIAN HEROES: THEN & NOW

DIETRICH BONHOEFFER

In the Midst of Wickedness

JANET & GEOFF BENGE

YWAM
PUBLISHING
P.O. BOX 55787 / SEATTLE, WA 98155

YWAM Publishing is the publishing ministry of Youth With A Mission (YWAM), an international missionary organization of Christians from many denominations dedicated to presenting Jesus Christ to this generation. To this end, YWAM has focused its efforts in three main areas: (1) training and equipping believers for their part in fulfilling the Great Commission (Matthew 28:19), (2) personal evangelism, and (3) mercy ministry (medical and relief work).

For a free catalog of books and materials, call (425) 771-1153 or (800) 922-2143. Visit us online at www.ywampublishing.com.

Dietrich Bonhoeffer: In the Midst of Wickedness

Published by YWAM Publishing
a ministry of Youth With A Mission
P.O. Box 55787, Seattle, WA 98155-0787

Library of Congress Cataloging-in-Publication Data

Benge, Janet, 1958–
   Dietrich Bonhoeffer : in the midst of wickedness / Janet Benge, Geoff Benge.
      p. cm. — (Christian heroes, then & now)
   Includes bibliographical references.
   ISBN 978-1-57658-713-3 (pbk.)
   1. Bonhoeffer, Dietrich, 1906–1945. 2. Theologians—Germany—Biography. I. Benge, Geoff, 1954– II. Title.
   BX4827.B57B355 2012
   230′.044092—dc23
   [B]   2012006860

Second printing 2015

Printed in the United States of America

CHRISTIAN HEROES: THEN & NOW

Available in paperback, e-book, and audiobook formats.
Unit Study Curriculum Guides are available for select biographies.
www.HeroesThenAndNow.com

1930s Germany

North Sea

Baltic Sea

DENMARK

East Prussia

HOLLAND

•Bremerhaven

Finkenwalde•

Berlin•

GERMANY

POLAND

• Friedrichsbrunn

Buchenwald
• Concentration
Camp

Breslau•

Flossenbürg
Concentration
Camp •

CZECHOSLOVAKIA

FRANCE

Tübingen•

Regensburg•

Schönberg•

Munich•
Ettal•

SWITZERLAND

AUSTRIA

HUNGARY

Contents

Chapter 1

Everything Had Changed

Eleven-year-old Dietrich Bonhoeffer groaned. It had been impossible to find food in Berlin that day, for any price, even on the black market. For days now it had been like this, and as his family's food forager, he was discouraged. Even *ersatz* (substitute food commodities) could not be found. No matter how hard Dietrich tried, he often came home empty-handed.

From the talk he heard on the streets, it was the British navy's fault. They were blockading Germany's ports on the Baltic Sea, cutting off the supply of food coming from abroad. On top of that, with so many young men away fighting, there were fewer people to farm the land and harvest crops in the country. And what food was available was usually used to feed the troops. As winter approached, the situation was getting even worse. The German potato supply was exhausted, and people were supposed to substitute turnips for potatoes. Dietrich could hardly believe it. In Germany turnips were used to feed horses and cows and pigs, and now people were expected to eat them. How could it be? The war wasn't supposed to have gone on this long. He thought it was only going to last a few months at most. Three years later, they were still fighting.

The war had changed everything. The once prosperous streets of Berlin were filled with soup kitchens where emaciated and bedraggled people lined up in the cold to await a ladleful of soup that seemed to be more water than anything else. And that wasn't the only change Dietrich had to confront. As he crossed the bridge on his way to school, almost every morning he would look down and see men on the riverbank trying to retrieve the body of some desperate person who had jumped from the bridge to their death. Just thinking about it sent a shiver down Dietrich's spine.

More than anything, Dietrich wanted things to be normal again. He wanted Berlin to be the happy, magical place it had been when his family moved to the city from Breslau.

Chapter 2

Berlin

W e're leaving Breslau today," six-year-old Dietrich Bonhoeffer said as he ran through the
nursery and joined Sabine, his twin sister, who was
peering out the window at the commotion below.

Sabine grinned. "I know. Just think, tomorrow
we'll wake up in Berlin!"

Dietrich was not sure whether or not that was a
good thing.

As the children stared out the nursery window,
their nanny, Maria Horn, walked briskly into the
room. Three-year-old Susanne trotted along behind
her. "Children, dress quickly and come downstairs
for breakfast and prayers," Maria said. "There is a lot
going on today, so look out for each other and mind
what you are told."

Dietrich nodded as he donned his blue silk under-shirt and white frock. He hoped that when he got to Berlin his mother would let him wear lederhosen like his three older brothers, Karl-Friedrich, Walter, and Klaus.

"Let me do your hair," Maria said. "Sabine, you first."

Dietrich stood quietly and watched as Maria braided his sister's thick black hair. Even though he and Sabine were twins, they did not look the least bit alike. Like the rest of the Bonhoeffer children, Sabine had dark hair and flashing brown eyes. Dietrich was the odd one out. He had the same bright blue eyes and white-blond hair as his mother. Often when they were on family outings, strangers assumed Dietrich was a friend and not even a member of the family.

Soon the entire family was seated in the dining room for breakfast. The heavy wooden table was arrayed with a loaf of rye bread, butter, cheese, wild raspberry jam, and Dietrich's favorite, hot cocoa.

Even though it was going to be a busy day, Diet-rich's mother, Paula, insisted on starting the day with a Bible story, family prayers, and the singing of a hymn. This was the way each day in Dietrich's life had begun so far, and he loved the way his mother could make Old Testament stories come alive. Today was no exception. All eight Bonhoeffer children sat mesmerized as their mother told of David's slingshot whirling above his head as he faced Goliath.

When breakfast and prayers were over, Dietrich and Sabine wandered around the grounds of their home one last time. Dietrich knew that the family was moving two hundred miles northwest to Berlin, Germany's capital, where his father, Karl Bonhoeffer, had a new job as head of Psychiatry and Neurology at the University of Berlin. Taking each other's hand, the twins walked down to the creek, where they had often gathered raspberries for the cook, and past the spot where they could count on seeing a dragonfly or two. They walked past the tennis court, where their favorite memories were not of tennis but of watching their older brothers and sisters ice-skate during the long winter months. It had been their father's suggestion to pour water on the tennis court and wait for it to freeze like an ice rink. Dietrich's two older sisters, Ursula and Christine, loved figure skating on the smooth, frozen surface.

Dietrich and Sabine walked into the wooded area where Dietrich and his older brothers had built forts and dug caves into the clay bank.

"I wish all the animals could come with us," Dietrich said wistfully as they climbed over the fence into the cook's garden.

"Me too," Sabine agreed. "But Mama says the family that's moving in wants to look after them for us."

As he thought about the room of the house where their mother allowed them to keep animals, Dietrich hoped this was the case. The room was filled with lively rabbits, guinea pigs, birds, lizards, and snakes, all kept in neat cages. Sometimes one of the creatures would escape, causing great excitement in the house.

Dietrich wondered what the new house in Berlin would be like. His mother had said that living in a big city would be quite different, but Fräulein Käthe Horn would still teach him and Sabine, so he had no need to be concerned about going off to school just yet.

A succession of horse-drawn carriages pulled up to the front of the Bonhoeffer house. Dietrich and Sabine headed toward them. Soon the whole family was seated in the carriages, and moments later they were off to the station to catch the train to Berlin. As the carriages pulled away, Dietrich took one last look at the only home he'd ever lived in. He would miss the rambling three-story house and the wonderful grounds with their beckoning adventures. He hoped his mother was right when she said that living in Berlin would be just as much fun.

The train trip was wonderful for Dietrich. He stuck his head out the window as the huge steam engine huffed its way out of the station. He watched as they left the buildings of Breslau behind and headed into the German countryside. It was late March, and signs of spring were everywhere. New leaves clung to the boughs of trees, flowers dotted pastures in which cows grazed, and the air rushing in through the window seemed to have a hint of sweet fragrance. When the train stopped at stations along the way, Dietrich watched as men and women climbed aboard. As the train began to fill with people, he listened to the adults' conversations. Some talked about the weather or what they intended to do in Berlin, while others talked about things happening in the German Republic and about Kaiser Wilhelm II.

Eventually the train puffed to a halt in Berlin. Trains were pulled up at platforms everywhere; Dietrich had never seen so many people coming and going. As he climbed down to the station platform, Dietrich was amazed by all the activity. But he wasn't sure whether he would like the city that lay beyond the railway station.

Dietrich need not have been concerned. He loved Berlin from the moment he arrived. With three million inhabitants, Berlin was the largest city he'd ever seen. The city had so many modern marvels: Europe's only open-air swimming pool for families and a cinema showing silent movies. It also had wide boulevards that converged at public squares with flower gardens, fountains, and statues.

The Bonhoeffer family settled into a home on Brückenalle, a wide, tree-lined street on the main route to Bellevue Train Station. The new house had three stories, just like the Breslau house, but it was much smaller and didn't have the spacious grounds of the family's previous residence. It had no space where Dietrich could roam and build forts. However, the new house did back up to a huge park that surrounded Bellevue Castle, home of the kaiser and his family. Dietrich and Sabine would peer through the railings at the young princes taking their morning walk. One day one of the little princes came right up to the fence and tried to poke Sabine with a stick. Sabine and Dietrich ran for cover.

The house on Brückenalle was not far from Friedrich-Werder Grammar School, where Dietrich's older brothers and sisters were enrolled. Dietrich was grateful he did not yet have to attend school. His parents had an unusual view of education. His mother would say, "I will not send my boys to school until I have to. Germany breaks the back of a young man twice, first at school, then in the military." In fact, Dietrich's mother had taught all five of the older children at home until they moved to Berlin. Even though she was from a wealthy family, as a young woman she had insisted on attending college to become a qualified schoolteacher.

While the five older children—Karl-Friedrich and Walter, both age thirteen; eleven-year-old Klaus; ten-year-old Ursula; and nine-year-old Christine—went off to school, the three youngest children, including Dietrich, continued to be taught at home by the Horn sisters. Both Käthe and Maria Horn had attended the Moravian school in Herrnhut that Dietrich's mother had attended. Count Zinzendorf, whom Dietrich heard a lot about from all three women, had founded the village in the mid-eighteenth century and used it as a place to preach that Christianity was about a personal relationship with God. That message caught fire in the hearts of the Moravians who migrated to live at Herrnhut and who became fearless missionaries, spreading the gospel from India to Jamaica.

Although Dietrich's father did not call himself a Christian, he supported the Christian atmosphere that surrounded the home. In Berlin, Dietrich's mother continued her practice of reading the Bible aloud and leading the family in prayer and hymn singing each morning. She also liked to talk about her father, who was once a chaplain to Kaiser Wilhelm II, the German emperor and King of Prussia and her brother, who was a local Lutheran pastor. Yet the Bonhoeffer family rarely attended church, and each of the children had been baptized at home.

Always curious, Dietrich found a lot to explore in Berlin. One of his favorite spots was the Berlin Zoo, which was only a short distance from the Brückenalle house. The zoo was the grandest in Europe, filled with all sorts of exotic animals: elephants, lions, giraffes, zebras, and other animals from Africa; tigers from Asia; kangaroos from Australia; and monkeys, baboons, gorillas, chimpanzees, and strange birds with colorful plumage from all over the world. Dietrich loved watching the animals in their cages. He also loved the zoo buildings: the Antelope House with its four minarets, the enormous Indian-inspired Elephant House, the Egyptian Ostrich House, the Japanese Wader House, the Chinese-inspired Elephant Gate, and the Arabian-style houses for the solipeds. Surrounding the zoo were numerous music pavilions and large restaurants with expansive terraces. Dietrich explored it all.

The remainder of 1912 passed quickly, and on February 4, 1913, Dietrich and Sabine celebrated their seventh birthday. It was the beginning of an eventful year. Dietrich's parents bought a summerhouse at Friedrichsbrunn, 120 miles southwest of Berlin in the Harz Mountains. Only Dietrich's father had visited the place when the younger children, the Horn sisters, two housemaids, and governess Fräulein Lenchen went off to prepare the new house for the family's summer vacation.

The group caught the train from Berlin to the town of Thale, where two horse-drawn carriages were waiting for them. Their baggage was loaded into one of the carriages, and everyone piled into the other for the four-mile trip to the summerhouse at Friedrichsbrunn.

Dietrich loved the new summerhouse. The two-story house had once been a foresters' lodge and was large and rambling. The housemaids set to work airing it out and getting a fire started in the fireplace while the children unpacked their bags. As darkness descended across the Harz Mountains, candles were lit in the rooms. After dinner, Maria Horn tucked the children into bed. Dietrich could hardly sleep. He was eager for morning to arrive so he could explore the surrounding forest and meadows.

The next morning Dietrich felt like he was visiting a fairy tale land, and for good reason. Many German fairy tales, including "Hansel and Gretel," "Sleeping Beauty," and "Little Red Riding Hood," were all local folk stories. Dietrich delighted in seeing the steep-roofed houses with their tiny crisscrossed windows and rounded wooden doors. Everything was enchanting: the narrow cobblestone streets, the dark forest, the silver mines. It was easy to imagine Snow White happening upon seven hardworking dwarfs or Hansel and Gretel finding themselves in front of a witch's door deep in the forest.

When the rest of the Bonhoeffer family arrived at Friedrichsbrunn, Dietrich and Sabine were waiting for them at the train station in Thale with all sorts of stories to tell their parents and older brothers and sisters.

After a wonderful time together at the summer-house, the family headed back to Berlin. Reluctantly Dietrich boarded the train for the journey home, leaving Friedrichsbrunn behind.

Back in Berlin, Dietrich's parents had some special news. Dietrich would be going to school the following week. His heart sank. Dietrich had been perfectly happy studying at home with Sabine and Susanne, and now he had to leave them behind and go off to school. For the first time in his life, he would be doing something by himself.

At first Dietrich hated school. Sitting at a desk all day was too restrictive, and he longed to be at home roaming around the house or playing in the yard. However, after a few months, he began looking forward to school each morning. Dietrich met new friends and managed to get top marks in all his subjects with little effort. Whenever he felt bored, he would think about the summer he had to look forward to in Friedrichsbrunn. He made plans for the games he would play there but had no idea how different that summer would be.

Chapter 3

At War

Look over there!" Dietrich exclaimed as he eyed a table laden with chocolate delicacies. The three youngest Bonhoeffer children ran to it.

"I love them all!" Susanne said as she examined the wonderful array of chocolate animals.

"Can we choose one each?" Dietrich asked Fräulein Lenchen.

"I think so," the governess said with a smile.

Soon Dietrich and his two sisters were nibbling on chocolate rabbits as they wandered among the stalls at the village fair. There was so much to see: rows of finches in cages, men clad in traditional lederhosen strolling by with quivers slung across their backs, pretty young girls and old women looking like characters in one of Friedrichsbrunn's many folk tales.

Dietrich and his sisters' favorite attraction was the merry-go-round, a large wooden wheel with seats at the end of each spoke. Eight children could sit on it at once while a white horse pulled it around and around. Dietrich helped Susanne climb into one of the seats. Once all three children were in place, off they went. The merry-go-round circled while the local band played music in the background. Every so often Dietrich would catch a glance of Fräulein Lenchen and Maria Horn, who were conversing with an older man. When the merry-go-round came to a stop, Fräulein Lenchen beckoned the children over. Dietrich noticed that the band had abruptly stopped playing.

"Quickly, children, we must go home," the governess exclaimed, tugging at Dietrich's shirt.

"But why? We're having so much fun," Dietrich queried.

Fräulein Lenchen shook her head. Her voice was low. "We cannot stay. Today Germany has declared war on Russia. Your parents will want you back in Berlin, where they know you're safe. We must pack immediately. When you are old, you'll never forget this day—August 1, 1914."

A thousand questions raced through Dietrich's head. He dared not ask one of them aloud. Why Russia? Would the war last long? The only wars he knew about were the Napoleonic wars and the Franco-Prussian War, which he had studied in school. Would this new war be like them? Would his father have to fight? What would all of this mean for the Bonhoeffers?

Twenty-four hours after leaving the fair, Dietrich, Sabine, and Susanne, along with their nanny and governess, were sitting on the train headed back to Berlin. The train was filled with young men traveling to Berlin to sign up for military service to fight for their country. At station after station as more young men boarded, girls threw flowers to them.

As the train rolled toward Berlin, Dietrich listened to the conversations around him. It sounded like Germany had declared war on both Russia and Serbia because an Austro-Hungarian prince had been assassinated on a visit to Sarajevo in Serbia one month before. As a result, the Austro-Hungarian Empire had declared war on Serbia and Russia, and since Kaiser Wilhelm II had promised to support the Austro-Hungarians, Germany also declared war on Russia and Serbia.

When the train pulled into the next station, the stationmaster walked the length of the train yelling the latest news. "We have invaded Luxembourg. Long live the kaiser!" Dietrich's heart beat fast with excitement, though he was also a little confused. He thought Germany was at war with Russia and Serbia, so why had they invaded Luxembourg? Luxembourg was nowhere near Russia. Still, Dietrich hoped the war would go on for a long time, long enough for him to grow up and join the fighting.

As the group made their way to the Bonhoeffer house on Brückenalle, they passed the kaiser's palace, where a crowd had gathered to sing patriotic songs and wave flags. The scene reminded Dietrich of the village fair the day before.

By the time Dietrich got home, he was excited. So was Sabine, who burst into the house and yelled excitedly, "Hurrah! There's a war!"

Paula Bonhoeffer swept into the entrance hall. "Don't ever celebrate war," she snapped. "Many good men will die before it is over."

Dietrich crept up to his bedroom. This was not the homecoming he'd expected. He looked out the window and could see groups of men continuing to sing patriotic songs as they walked arm in arm down the street.

While his parents maintained a cautious view of the war, Dietrich's three older brothers were caught up in the excitement. Karl-Friedrich, Walter, and Klaus already had a map up on the wall in Walter's room on which they kept track of the German army's advance, using colored pins to represent the various battalions of troops. The map already had pins in Luxembourg, and the next day Germany declared war on France. By the following day, August 4, 1914, German troops had entered Belgium. Walter, who was particularly patient with Dietrich's questions about what was happening, explained that German troops were on a rapid advance through Belgium on their way to outflank the French army and capture Paris. When he finished his explanation, he pressed several pins into Belgium on the map. Germany was at war not only with Russia and Serbia but now also with France. According to Dietrich's brothers, the war would be over in a matter of weeks, with a great victory for Germany.

By the end of the day on August 4, Dietrich learned that things had taken a turn. Belgium was a neutral country, and because Germany had violated its neutrality, Great Britain had declared war on Germany and Austria-Hungary. Walter explained that this turn of events was a surprise. After all, Kaiser Wilhelm II and King George V of England were cousins, though another cousin of the kaiser's, Alix, was married to Tsar Nicholas II of Russia, and Germany had declared war on Russia.

Within a week of the family's return to Berlin, Europe was in an uproar. British soldiers were already confronting German troops in Belgium and northern France, and Dietrich learned that far away in North America, Canada was preparing to send troops to fight alongside the British and the French. It seemed to Dietrich that everyone breathed a sigh of relief when President Woodrow Wilson of the United States vowed that his country would not enter the war.

The Bonhoeffer boys read accounts of battles and continued to mark German progress with pins on the map, though they grumbled to each other that this was nowhere as exciting as being in the middle of those battles. They longed to go and fight, but that seemed unlikely, since Karl-Friedrich, the oldest, was only fifteen years old. He told his brothers that the war would not drag on for three years until he was old enough to put on a uniform and fight.

Apart from the newspaper headlines and the soldiers marching through the streets of Berlin on their way to fight, the Bonhoeffer household was not disrupted much. Dietrich started piano lessons and soon became an excellent pianist. He loved hearing how his grandmother, his mother's mother, Countess Kalckreuth, had been a wonderful pianist. She had taken lessons from Clara Schumann, one of Germany's most distinguished pianists and the wife of composer Robert Schumann.

The entire Bonhoeffer family was musical and often had family musical evenings during which everyone played an instrument or sang. Like Dietrich, Karl-Friedrich played the piano. Walter played the violin and Klaus the cello, while Christine, Ursula, and Mrs. Bonhoeffer sang arias.

Conversation at the dinner table normally centered on music and sometimes schoolwork. Occasionally, but not often, the war encroached on the family's dinner conversation. On one occasion Fräulein Lenchen brought Sabine a brooch with the words "Now we'll thrash them!" engraved on it. At dinner Karl Bonhoeffer saw the ornamental pin his daughter was wearing and said, "What have we here? Take it off and give it to me, please." Sabine took it off and handed it over. Dietrich watched as their father dropped the jewelry into his pocket. Sabine opened her mouth to protest and then closed it. Dietrich understood; it was not wise to argue with Papa.

"Don't worry about it," Paula reassured her daughter. "I'll find you a prettier brooch to wear."

It didn't take long for Dietrich and Sabine to begin to appreciate their parents' point of view. War was not fun and was not something to celebrate. Within weeks of the start of fighting, one of Dietrich's cousins was killed, then another, and then a third had his eye shot out and his leg crushed. As the casualty count from the war continued to rise, the Bonhoeffer household, like many others in Berlin, became quiet. Everyone had a lot of time for thinking and reflecting. Dietrich and Sabine felt it too. They shared a bedroom, and at night when the light was turned off, they often talked about how scary war was. They also discussed questions about dying and God, and for months the two of them made a pact to drift off to sleep thinking about the word *eternity* and nothing else.

Apart from soldiers in the streets and news of increasing casualties, the first signs of the war in Berlin were small things. Regular wheat bread was replaced with *kriegsbrot*, war bread, which had potato meal added to make the rye and wheat go farther. Dietrich didn't mind the taste, and the bread lasted for a week without getting stale. Meat, eggs, and butter began to get scarce as the German government began to control the food production of the country. Special laws were passed that limited how farmers could produce and slaughter animals.

Although Dietrich was too young to fight, everything happening around him made him restless. He longed for an adventure of his own, and so he appointed himself the family scavenger. Even though he was only nine years old, he often slipped out of the house to look for food to buy on the black market. Sometimes he came home with mutton fat and watched as the cook deftly created "lamb chops" using it. The cook would boil rice that she then formed into shapes like a chop. A wooden skewer was stuck into the chop-shaped rice to serve as a bone. The aroma of mutton wafted through the house as the rice chops were fried in mutton fat. To Dietrich's surprise, the end result tasted quite like the lamb chops the family had enjoyed before the war. The chops were served with green peas and a sprig of watercress, and Karl declared it impossible to tell the difference. However, the cook's attempts at vegetable "beef steaks" did not go so well. The steaks had a lot of spinach in them, and Dietrich could not get past the green color once he cut into the "steak."

Dietrich continued attending school, and from the map in Walter's room, he regularly kept up with the events on the battlefield. As 1915 rolled on, it felt to Dietrich as though the war had been going on forever. More cousins and family friends were wounded or killed in the fighting, and despite Dietrich's best efforts, food was getting harder to find. And there was one word in Germany that everyone was beginning to tire of hearing—*ersatz* (substitute). Germany had three allies in the war: the Austro-Hungarian Empire, the Ottoman Empire, and Bulgaria. Apart from the border Germany shared with the Austro-Hungarian Empire, the country's other six borders were all shared with declared enemies. This made it difficult to bring food and clothing into the country from the north, east, or west.

Dietrich knew that coffee was certainly not coming into Germany. His father loved a strong, black cup of coffee each morning, but before long Karl resorted to drinking ersatz coffee made of roasted barley and oats and chemicals extracted from coal tar. When the government found a more pressing use for the barley, ersatz coffee was made from roasted acorns and beechnuts. When the acorns began to be in short supply, carrots and turnips were used. This was a long way from tasting anything like real coffee, but Dietrich's father still drank a cup of it every morning while reading the newspaper.

The end of 1915 brought more shortages besides food. Posters appeared all over Berlin with the words *Sparsamkeit, Erhaltung, Wiederverwerten*—Thrift, Conservation, Recycling. Germans were urged to drop off old woolen garments to be cut up, dyed, and made into uniforms for the troops. Animal pelts, even rabbit pelts, were requested for the lining of coats, and housewives were asked to give up their copper and brass pots to make ammunition. Church bells were taken out of steeples and melted down to make cannons. Nickel coins were melted and replaced with iron ones.

The war dragged on into 1916, and Dietrich could see from Walter's map that neither side was moving much. The German army and the Allies (Great Britain, Russia, France, Serbia, and Belgium) seemed to be stalled along a line from Switzerland through eastern France and Belgium to the North Sea. In mid-February 1916, German forces mounted a massive attack at Verdun in France. Walter explained to Dietrich that the German plan was to break through Allied lines and once and for all gain the advantage on the Western Front, as the battle line in France and Belgium was called. And while there was a Western Front, from Walter's map Dietrich could see that there was also an Eastern Front where German forces were fighting.

In March 1916, Dietrich's parents moved from the house on Brückenalle to 14 Wangenheimstrasse in the suburb of Grunewald, near the Halensee railroad station. Although the large new house was in a well-to-do area of town, its main attraction was the acre of land surrounding it, which the family plowed and gardened. The family also kept a goat for milk. Dietrich loved the new location and enjoyed milking the goat. He saved his pocket money and bought a hen for the family. He felt a surge of pride when he collected eggs from the henhouse.

As July 1916 rolled around, the German victory and breakthrough of the Allied lines at Verdun had not occurred. The pins still had not moved on Walter's map. Instead, after five months of fighting, the battle ground was in a stalemate, with three hundred thousand German soldiers dead. Dietrich was glad to leave Berlin and all the bad news behind and head with the rest of the family to the summerhouse at Friedrichsbrunn. With the sun shining and crystal-clear water bubbling over the rocks in the stream, it was easy to forget that Europe was in turmoil.

While at Friedrichsbrunn, Dietrich and Sabine spent hours walking through the woods and across the mountain meadows gathering wild mushrooms and strawberries, which the cook dried and packed into bags to take back to Berlin for the winter ahead.

Before long, the shadows across the Harz Mountains were getting longer and the days shorter. Dietrich knew it was time to pack up everything and head back to Berlin. He hated to leave. In the peace and quiet of the mountains, he'd almost forgotten that Germany was at war.

Chapter 4

Shadows

Back in Berlin, Dietrich returned to school. Things were getting grimmer. Dietrich's father explained this was because of the number of casualties Germany was suffering on both the Eastern and Western Fronts. Everyone seemed to know someone whose relative or friend had been killed or severely wounded.

To make matters worse, food was in even shorter supply. Even ersatz commodities were hard to come by. The British navy was blockading German ports on the Baltic Sea, stopping supplies of food and other necessities from being imported. With so many young men away fighting, fewer people were available to farm the land and harvest the crops. What food was available was usually directed toward the troops.

Dietrich tried to rustle up as much to eat as he could, but some days it was impossible, even on the black market, at any price. He was thankful for the garden and the goat and hen at home. They might not be much, but they provided the family with something to eat.

As winter approached, things got even worse. The German potato supply was exhausted, and turnips were substituted for potatoes. Dietrich, like most Germans, found this hard to accept. Turnips were feed for horses, cows, and pigs, and now people were supposed to eat them. This was outrageous, but gnawing hunger trumped the outrage of the people. Even Dietrich found himself looking forward to boiled turnips.

Hunger grew in Germany, and as Dietrich moved about the city, he noticed that soup kitchens were opening everywhere to feed the starving. Dietrich watched as emaciated, bedraggled people lined up in the cold to wait for a ladleful of soup that appeared to him to be more water than anything else. He listened as the people complained that farmers were keeping the food they grew on their farms for themselves.

Hunger and flagging morale among Germans caused Dietrich to confront another side effect of the war—suicide. On his way to and from school he had to cross a bridge, and almost every morning as he crossed, Dietrich would look down and see a group of men on the riverbank. He soon learned the men were trying to retrieve the body of someone who had jumped from the bridge to his death. No matter how many times he saw the scene, each time Dietrich felt a shiver run down his spine.

Despite the difficulties Germany faced, spirits remained high in the Bonhoeffer household as 1917 arrived. Dietrich continued to study hard at school and practice the piano. He even began experimenting with writing his own compositions. Family music nights remained one of his favorite times. Another highlight occurred on his and Sabine's birthday on February 4, when they turned eleven. As a birthday present, Dietrich was given an egg, which the cook had beaten with sugar for him to drink. Dietrich savored every drop of the whipped liquid.

Nineteen seventeen was also the year that both of his older brothers, Karl-Friedrich and Walter, turned eighteen, old enough to be drafted into the army. Karl-Friedrich, who was eleven months older than Walter, was the first to be called up. He chose to join the Fifth Regiment of the Guards at Spandau and underwent military training. Because he had been planning to attend university to study physics, he slipped his physics textbook into his knapsack before leaving for the Western Front. Dietrich could tell that his parents were sad to see Karl-Friedrich leave. Walter could hardly wait *his* turn to enlist in the army. He prepared himself for combat by taking long hikes carrying a heavy backpack.

Meanwhile, news reached Berlin of happenings to the east in Russia. As Karl Bonhoeffer read the newspaper, he explained to Dietrich that Russia was in political turmoil. On March 17 news came that because of the turmoil, Tsar Nicholas II of Russia had abdicated the throne. Dietrich and his father hoped this would mean good news for Germany and the war with Russia.

Less than a month later, however, on April 6, there was some bad news. The United States had declared war on Germany and would be sending troops to fight alongside the Allies on the Western Front. Walter explained to Dietrich that while this was bad news, the United States had a fairly small army, and it would take months for them to train enough soldiers to send to fight in France and Belgium. Walter was sure that by the time the soldiers arrived, the war would be over, with a victory for Germany. He only hoped it would last long enough for him to go and fight.

Once again the Bonhoeffer family headed to the summerhouse at Friedrichsbrunn, even taking the goat with them on the train so they would have fresh milk over the summer. Again Dietrich basked in the peace and quiet of the Harz Mountains. But while Berlin and the war seemed far off, he did not forget food scavenging. Mushrooms were plentiful in the mountains, and Dietrich spent his days, usually with Sabine, gathering as many mushrooms as possible for the cook to dry and take back to Berlin at the end of summer. He and Sabine also gathered wild strawberries that were made into thick jam and packed in jars, also to be taken back to Berlin.

As usual, summer seemed to race by too fast for Dietrich, who soon was on the train back to Berlin.

Dietrich returned to school and excelled in all his subjects except handwriting, which his teachers deemed to be messy and in need of improvement.

In November, Germany received good news. In Russia a revolution had occurred, and now the Communist Bolsheviks, led by Vladimir Lenin, ruled the country and wanted an armistice (an agreement to pause fighting) with Germany. There was great excitement. The Germans had beaten the Russians, and now they could turn their full attention to the Western Front and crush France, Great Britain, and the Allies.

There was excitement in the Bonhoeffer home as well. The war was still being fought when Walter turned eighteen on December 10. He would get his chance to go and fight for his country after all. Like Karl-Friedrich, Walter chose to join the Fifth Regiment of the Guards at Spandau and went off to train as a soldier.

On February 4, 1918, while Walter was still away training to fight, Dietrich celebrated his twelfth birthday. He marveled at how things had changed from his previous birthday. Then, things had been grim and German morale low. Now, with a signed armistice with Russia, there was optimism in the air; five hundred thousand German soldiers who had fought the Russians were now being transferred to the Western Front to strengthen German forces there. With these reinforcements, everyone expected General Luderndorf, the German chief of staff, to mount a massive attack on the Allies and win the war for

Germany. Victory seemed at hand. At least Dietrich hoped so, because he'd grown tired of the war and the effect it had on everyday life.

Sure enough, on March 21, 1918, General Luderndorf launched the German attack. So successful were the first days of the attack that on March 24, Kaiser Wilhelm II ordered a national holiday to celebrate. Dietrich, like most Germans, assumed the war was all but over. His father, however, was not so sure. How many times had Germans been told victory in the war was at hand, only to be disappointed? Even Dietrich conceded that his father had a point. But not Walter, who arrived home to spend time with the family after finishing military training and before heading to the Western Front. He saw things differently. Momentum in the war now favored Germany, especially with the reinforcements sent from the Eastern Front. These extra soldiers were more than enough to counteract the effect of the American soldiers who had begun arriving in France to fight.

It was only two weeks before Walter was to depart for the Western Front, and in early April the entire Bonhoeffer family made plans for a big send-off party. For his part, Dietrich composed an arrangement for the popular song, "Now, at last, we say Godspeed you on your journey."

When the night of the party arrived, many of Dietrich's relatives came to say farewell to Walter. They brought gifts and poems and songs. Dietrich sang his new musical arrangement while accompanying himself on the piano. It was well after midnight when the family went to bed. They were up early the next morning to take Walter to the train station. Dietrich felt envious as he shook his brother's hand. He hoped that Walter would come back a hero. He noticed tears rolling down his mother's cheeks as she hugged Walter good-bye on the crowded station platform.

Soon the steam locomotive began belching black smoke, and a whistle sounded. Walter jumped aboard the train and took a seat by the window. As the train slowly chugged away from the station platform, Dietrich's mother ran alongside and yelled, "Good-bye, Walter. Remember, it's only space that separates us."

Two weeks later, Dietrich was getting ready for school when the doorbell rang. Curious to know who it was so early in the morning, he ran downstairs just in time to see a messenger hand a telegram to his father. As Dietrich's father slipped the telegram from the envelope and read it, his face turned ashen. He walked into his study, closing the heavy wooden door behind him. A few moments later he left his study and laboriously climbed the stairs in silence. Normally Dietrich's father bounded up the stairs, but it seemed to Dietrich that today he was pulling himself up. His knuckles were white as he gripped the banister tightly for support. Dietrich began to tremble as he watched his father slowly climb the stairs. He knew something terrible had happened.

It was hours before Dietrich's father appeared from the bedroom where his mother had still been in bed. When he appeared, his face was still ashen. "It was news of your brother Walter," he told Dietrich and the other children in a halting voice. "He is dead from a shrapnel wound."

Dietrich stood motionless, trying to comprehend his father's words. Dead from an exploded bomb? How could it be? Just two weeks before, Walter had climbed onto the train grinning and waving and looking toward the future. Now it was over for him forever. Even though Dietrich knew that other German soldiers, hundreds of thousands of them, had been killed in the fighting, he could not imagine that his older brother was one of them and gone for good.

To make matters more unbearable for the family, a letter soon arrived from Walter, dictated three hours before the time the telegram said he had died. It read:

My dears,

Today I had the second operation, and I must admit that it went far less pleasantly than the first because the splinters that were removed were deeper. Afterwards I had to have two camphor injections with an interval between them, but I hope that this is the end of the matter. I am using my technique of thinking of other things so as not to think of the pain. There are more interesting things in the world just now than my wounds. Mount Kemmel and its possible consequences, and today's news of the taking of Ypres, give us great cause for hope. I dare not think about my poor regiment, so severely did it suffer in the last few days. How are things going with the other officer cadets? I think of you with long-ing, my dears, every minute of the long days and nights.

From so far away,
Your Walter

The letter was more than Dietrich's mother could bear. Paula sobbed until her eyes were swollen shut, and the next morning she did not come down to breakfast. As if the death of her son were not enough, Paula learned that her son Klaus, although only sev-enteen years old, had been called up to serve in the army.

Dietrich could see that this was an unbearable blow to his mother, who began spending long periods of each day in her bedroom. He would often hear her sobbing. In fact, the children saw little of their mother as she shuttered herself away in her room. Then one night at dinner their father quietly announced, "Your mother needs a break. She has gone to stay with the Schönes. One day soon you'll be able to visit her."

Dietrich looked around the table. His siblings looked as confused as he felt. His mother would be living next door with the neighbors, and he would not be able to see her. Despite his confusion, he trusted that his father knew what was best for their mother.

The Bonhoeffer children continued on without their mother around. After a few weeks they were able to visit her for brief periods. Sometimes when

Dietrich visited, she would stare blankly at the wall, and at other times she made the effort to talk to him. He knew better than to mention Walter's name to her, or to his father, for that matter. When someone outside the family spoke of Walter to their father, Karl would quietly get up and leave the room.

Thankfully Klaus wasn't sent to fight in the thick of the battle on the Western Front. Instead he was assigned as an orderly at German General Headquarters in Spa, Belgium.

Walter's death and the absence of his two older brothers who were serving in the army left a hole in Dietrich's life. He had no one with whom he could discuss the war and his feelings about it except Sabine and Susanne.

As summer approached, Paula Bonhoeffer could not bear to think of the children going to Friedrichsbrunn without Walter. Instead, Dietrich, Sabine, and Susanne were sent with Maria and Käthe Horn to vacation in Boltenhagen. Dietrich and his two sisters relaxed at the seaside resort on the Baltic Sea and tried to forget all that had happened to the family in the past few weeks. Dietrich also spent time sitting in a wicker chair on the beach reading, and built elaborate sand castles with his sisters.

While at the beach one day, Dietrich watched two military seaplanes perform maneuvers above the beach. It was a wonderful sight as the planes looped and turned in the air. Then to Dietrich's horror, one of the seaplanes suddenly nose-dived toward the beach and crashed, sending a plume of black smoke high

into the air. Dietrich knew that the force of the crash
was so great that the pilot would have been killed.
He knew that the pilot wasn't just a pilot but also
someone's son, as was Walter. It seemed to Dietrich
that wherever you went in Germany these days,
death followed.

Back in Berlin after the vacation, Dietrich was
relieved to learn that his mother was no longer staying with the Schönes. She was back at the Bonhoeffer
home. Yet Dietrich could see she was not the same as
before Walter's death. Shadows seemed to blot out
her smile. She was unable to run the house as she
had and constantly fretted about Karl-Friedrich and
Klaus.

Dietrich lived in fear that one of his other brothers
would be killed. He didn't know what would become
of his mother if that happened. Despite reports in
the newspapers of German successes on the Western Front, the massive military offensive that was
launched with the promise of winning the war for
Germany had ground to a halt. It seemed to Dietrich
that Germany was incapable of winning the war.

As the war dragged on, Berliners were asked to
make more sacrifices. Coal was in such short supply
that the Bonhoeffers closed off most of the house,
keeping only two rooms heated—the kitchen, where
they ate and talked, and the living room, where they
read and studied.

Things in Germany began changing quickly in
October 1918. The German naval commander in
the port of Kiel on the Baltic Sea decided to attack

the British navy and break their blockade of Germany's ports that was causing so much hardship in the nation. The British had a formidable naval force blockading Germany, and when the German navy was ordered to put to sea and attack the British, the sailors mutinied. To them, attacking the British navy was suicide, and they wouldn't take part in the foolhardy plan. Instead of putting to sea, they killed a number of fellow officers and took over their ships. Fearing that soldiers might join the side of the mutineers, the kaiser decided not to send in the army to crush the rebellion.

News of the mutiny spread throughout Germany. Dietrich wondered what it would mean for the country. His father reassured him that it was too early to tell. They would have to wait and see. They didn't have to wait long. The mutiny set off a wave of pent-up anger across Germany. The kaiser had been right to be concerned about the army because they also began to rebel against their leaders. They'd had enough of the endless fighting that produced nothing but dead and wounded soldiers. It was not just sailors and soldiers who'd had enough of the privations and destruction of war. Demonstrations began taking place all over Germany as workers went on strike. Berlin was a hotbed of such protests, and it wasn't uncommon for Dietrich to see groups of protestors marching and shouting in the streets. Sometimes the protesters' anger frightened him.

By the time November arrived, many German cities had been taken over by councils made up of workers and soldiers. Dietrich's father was concerned about the situation, which was beginning to resemble the situation in Russia the year before when the communists took over the country. Politicians began to fear a communist takeover of Germany.

Dietrich tried keeping up with the fast-changing situation, but he couldn't understand it all. It seemed that so many different groups were vying for control of Germany.

Early on the morning of November 10, 1918, Dietrich and Sabine heard Maria Horn sobbing in her room. They knocked on the door and entered the chilly bedroom. Maria lay on the bed, a piece of paper in her hand. She looked up at Dietrich and Sabine and cried, "It's over! The kaiser has abdicated. The war is lost. We are nothing."

Dietrich couldn't think of anything to say to comfort Maria and quietly left the room, followed by Sabine.

"So we've lost, Dietrich?" Sabine asked hesitantly. "Is it possible?"

"We'll have to ask Father," Dietrich replied.

The children found their father at the dining table reading a copy of the *Vossische Zeitung* newspaper.

"Is it true the kaiser has abdicated?" Dietrich asked.

Karl Bonhoeffer nodded. "Yes, yes, he abdicated yesterday. Already it says in the newspaper he is fleeing to exile in Holland."

"What does this mean, Papa?" Dietrich asked.

"I wish I could tell you. Friedrich Ebert and the Social Democratic Party have announced that Germany is now a republic, with a government led by a civilian and not by the kaiser, and the Reichstag will run this new republic. I'm not sure what this will mean for Germany. The Spartacists (communists) refuse to accept the new republic. I fear things might get worse in the country before they get better."

"And the war, Papa?"

"Ah, that is lost now," Karl sighed.

Sure enough, the following day, November 11, 1918, an armistice was declared with the Allies. The war was indeed over, and Germany had lost.

While the end of the war was a relief, it was also a bitter moment, a hard one for Germans, including Dietrich, to comprehend. In just two months Germany had gone from being a fighting nation to a defeated foe, from a nation led by an emperor—Kaiser Wilhelm II—to one led by a politician. And then there was the staggering casualty count. The four-year-long war had left over two million of Germany's brightest and bravest young men dead, among them Walter Bonhoeffer. Another four million had been wounded, left without legs or arms, blind, or shell-shocked. The numbers were so large Dietrich could scarcely comprehend them.

Dietrich was eight when the war started. Now he was twelve. He had few memories left of the peaceful Germany before the fighting. The old, genteel Germany his parents and grandparents inhabited had been swept away forever. Once Germany's future had been assured. Now Dietrich wasn't so sure. What would Germany be like when he grew up? No one, not even his father, could say.

Chapter 5

Theologian

By the start of 1919, Germany was in an uproar. The Council of People's Commissioners, under the leadership of Friedrich Ebert, now ruled the country. However, they didn't have the support of all German people, despite the fact that they had issued many decrees aimed at improving the lot of the population. As a result, rebellion seemed to be everywhere in Germany's cities, and Berlin was no exception. While Dietrich didn't fully understand the political maneuvering going on in the country, he often came across demonstrations and raging street battles as he made his way to and from school.

Things became quite dangerous in Berlin as the Spartacists (communists) battled in the streets to overthrow the Council of People's Commissioners and establish a government like the one that had taken over Russia in 1917. One of these battles took place in front of Halensee train station, a half-mile from the Bonhoeffer home. As night fell, Dietrich lay in bed listening to the screaming and yelling in the distance while the sound of gunfire peppered the air. He wondered whether things would ever settle down in Berlin.

It wasn't long before a paramilitary group of volunteer soldiers called Freikorps—many of whom had recently returned from the Western Front—decided to deal with the Spartacist uprising in Berlin. Bloody street battles were soon taking place, where people were shot or bludgeoned to death. Eventually the Freikorps prevailed, crushing the communist revolt and killing the two Spartacist leaders, Rosa Luxemburg and Karl Liebknecht, on January 15.

Although things settled down a little more on the streets of Berlin after this, many people were unhappy. As far as they could see, when they looked at the political and economic mess in Germany, the only answer to the nation's woes was communism. Dietrich knew that his father was not one who thought this way. Dietrich's father put his faith in the upcoming election of a new National Assembly as the way to stabilize the country.

The election took place on January 19, and the Social Democratic Party won a majority of the seats in the National Assembly. Their first job was to write a new democratic constitution for Germany. But as more violence erupted in Berlin's streets, the National

Assembly decided to convene in the city of Weimar to discuss drawing up the new constitution.

Meanwhile, Karl-Friedrich returned home. He had been wounded in the closing days of the war. Thankfully his injuries were not life threatening, though he did have to spend time in the hospital. Dietrich was glad when his oldest brother arrived home safely.

Karl-Friedrich told Dietrich stories about what it had really been like fighting on the Western Front. Before he left to go to war, Walter had made fighting seem almost glamorous, but Karl-Friedrich's grim description of conditions on the front lines painted a very different picture.

Soon Klaus also returned home. His military experience had been quite different from his older brother's. Klaus had been an orderly at German General Headquarters in Spa, Belgium, where conditions were much better than on the front lines. Klaus told Dietrich all about how he had been stationed in the hallway outside the room where Field Marshal von Hindenburg had met with Kaiser Wilhelm II and told him that for the good of Germany he must abdicate the throne. Klaus had witnessed history that day, he told Dietrich.

Except for Walter's absence, the Bonhoeffer family felt complete and happy again. Dietrich wished that all Germany could feel that way, but the country was far from happy or complete. As the debate over the new constitution dragged on in Weimar, fighting continued in the streets of various German cities.

In Munich a Soviet-style republic was declared, but once again the Freikorps moved in to brutally put the rebellion down.

It wasn't only left-wing groups like the communists and the socialists causing problems in the streets. Militant right-wing groups made up of workers and returned soldiers loyal to the old political order argued that Germany had lost the war because communists had fomented rebellion among the armed forces and stabbed the country in the back. These groups opposed both the new democratic order that had been established in Germany and the communists, whom they openly attacked in the streets.

At night Dietrich would lie in bed and think about the situation in Germany. Everyone seemed to blame someone else for the country's problems. Dietrich wondered how long people would continue to do this. Couldn't they see that their actions were only hurting Germany more?

There was more pain to come. In May 1919 the Allies published their postwar demands of Germany. The demands sent Germans reeling. Karl Bonhoeffer was so astonished he could hardly discuss the matter without sinking his face in his hands.

The Treaty of Versailles, a document named after the town in France where it was negotiated, asked a lot of a country that had already lost its kaiser, its sense of honor, and two million of its young men in the fighting. Now, according to the treaty, Germany must also give up territory to France, Belgium, and Denmark, along with all its Asian and African colonies. And if that were not enough, Article 231 of the treaty read, "The Allied and Associated Governments affirm and Germany accepts the responsibility of Germany and her allies for causing all the loss and damage to which the Allied and Associated Governments and their nationals have been subjected as a consequence of the war imposed upon them by the aggression of Germany and her allies." As a result of this article, Germany would be required to pay huge sums of money as reparations for the damage caused to the Allies during the war.

It was almost too much for Germany to accept, but what choice did the country have? Even Dietrich thought Article 231 went too far and railed against it. But in the end, Germany accepted the conditions and signed the Treaty of Versailles.

Around the same time, Dietrich began attending a new school, the Grunewald Gymnasium, designed to prepare students for a university education. The new school was located within easy walking distance of the Bonhoeffer home. No longer did Dietrich have to travel across Berlin to get to and from school. From the start, Dietrich enjoyed Grunewald Gymnasium, where he made new friends.

The teachers expected Dietrich to excel in science as his older brothers had when they attended. But Dietrich had a secret dream—he wanted to be a theologian. He knew it was a strange choice for a boy whose father was a well-known psychiatrist and who came from a family that did not attend church. But for some reason this was the vocation Dietrich felt drawn to, though he decided not to announce his decision to his family right away.

The new German constitution was finally agreed upon and was adopted on August 11. The new German republic was known as the Weimar Republic, after Weimar, where the new constitution was drafted. Dietrich hoped that things would settle down, but violence continued in the streets and constant attempts were made to overthrow the government.

Dietrich and Sabine celebrated their fourteenth birthday on February 4, 1920. Dietrich decided it was time to tell the family of his desire to become a theologian. He didn't think they would be supportive of his choice, and he was right. When his father heard the news, he raised his left eyebrow and kept a serious look on his face. Dietrich knew this was not good. Karl wanted to know why on earth his son had chosen theology and not science or music. Dietrich was a gifted piano player. Why not be a concert pianist rather than a theologian? Even Dietrich's mother, whose father and brother were both pastors, found Dietrich's career choice surprising. And his older brothers and sisters kidded him mercilessly about the decision. Karl-Friedrich wanted to know why Dietrich would want to leave the verifiable reality of science to escape in the fog of metaphysics. Besides, didn't he know that being a theologian was a dead-end career choice meant for lesser people than a Bonhoeffer? Klaus mockingly asked, "Why would you devote yourself to a poor, feeble, boring, and bourgeois institution as the church?" Dietrich confidently refuted his brother's question by saying, "In that case, I shall reform it!"

Dietrich stood his ground amid his family's opposition and skepticism. He could not satisfactorily explain the decision to himself, let alone his family, but he knew it was the right choice for him.

Although the Bonhoeffer family did not regularly attend church, all of the older children were confirmed in the Lutheran Church. Now that they were fourteen, Dietrich and Sabine were enrolled in confirmation class at the Grunewald church. In March 1920, Dietrich and Sabine were confirmed. Dietrich's mother gave him his brother Walter's Bible, which Dietrich treasured. He was honored to have the Bible and promised himself that he would read it often. At school, in preparation for his new career, Dietrich enrolled in Hebrew class and added Greek the following year.

Despite the constant ribbing from his older siblings, Dietrich found that Sabine and Susanne were more supportive of him. The "three little ones" had always had a kind of secret religious club. As small children they played "baptism," taking turns preaching sermons to each other. As they got older, they began walking to church together, even though their mother suggested that too much church might not be a good thing.

In November 1921, General Bramwell Booth of the Salvation Army arrived in Berlin to hold a series of evangelistic meetings. Until this point in his life, Dietrich had attended only the state church. He wondered how different the Salvation Army could possibly be.

Dietrich made his way to the hall where the meetings were being held. The thousands of people who showed up for the event surprised him, though he decided he was probably the youngest one there. The first thing he noticed as the meeting began was how different the music was. The songs were cheery and fast paced, and the singing was accompanied by a brass band as the congregation sang. How different this was from the Lutheran church.

Bramwell Booth, an elderly Englishman with white hair and a kindly smile, walked to the podium. He opened his Bible and, staring out at the crowd, began to preach about the kingdom of God and how there were no barriers between Christians from different countries. "Every land is my fatherland, for all lands are my Father's," he proclaimed. Dietrich was impressed, both by the message Booth preached and by the plain, unadorned, yet powerful way he delivered it. It was as though he could feel Booth's words as he spoke—something he had never felt before.

Dietrich told Sabine all about the meeting—the exuberant singing, the powerful preaching, and how afterward people had walked to the front in a public show that they wanted to become Christians. Dietrich had never seen anything like it.

Throughout this time Germany continued to be riven with violence. Left-wing groups continued agitating and fighting in the streets to see Germany become communist. They were opposed by ultranationalist right-wing groups wanting to turn back the clock to the way Germany used to be. They believed it was the communists, with the help of the Jews, who had undermined Germany's war effort and caused the country to lose the war. Many of these right-wing groups said that Germany should get rid of all its communists and Jews. Both the left-wing and right-wing groups took aim at the centrist Weimar government in Berlin.

Dietrich tried to avoid the violence and uncertainty in Germany by studying hard at school. However, as much as he tried to stay clear of the violence, on June 24, 1922, the violence followed him. While sitting in math class, Dietrich heard the crackle of gunfire outside. A small explosion followed and then the sound of a car engine revving and tires screeching. Dietrich knew this meant trouble. Sure enough, word filtered back that Walther Rathenau, Germany's foreign minister, had just been assassinated less than three hundred meters from Grunewald Gymnasium. Dietrich knew enough about what was going on in the country to know why Rathenau had been targeted. Rathenau was not only Jewish but had also advocated that Germany agree to the terms of the Treaty of Versailles. His was a position that right-wing groups hated, and they despised Rathenau.

At home, Dietrich learned from the newspaper that three members of a right-wing group had assassinated Rathenau. The men had pulled their car alongside his as he passed Grunewald Gymnasium and opened fire with a machine gun. They had then lobbed a hand grenade into the car before speeding away. When the police caught up to the assassins, the two who had fired the machine gun committed suicide, though the driver was arrested and would stand trial for his actions.

It was a sad day for Germany, and it was a sad day for Dietrich. Ursula Andreae, one of his friends at school, was Walther Rathenau's niece. Dietrich had often dined at her house with her uncle, a brilliant man, in attendance. Now the man was dead.

Despite such senseless violence, Dietrich moved forward with his life. In March 1923, at the age of seventeen, he passed the Abitur, or final examination, and was finished with high school. Not only did Dietrich pass the Abitur, but he also graduated with top grades in all his subjects, except handwriting, which was still declared "unsatisfactory." Now Dietrich looked forward to attending university.

Sabine chose to stay in Berlin and attend art school while Dietrich enrolled at the University of Tübingen, 325 miles southwest of Berlin. Karl-Friedrich had just earned his degree from that university and won a prestigious place at the Kaiser Wilhelm Institute in Berlin to study natural science. Klaus was also at Tübingen, as was Christine, a year behind her older brother and studying biology.

At the time, because money was short, it was arranged for Dietrich and Christine to stay with their

Grandmother Bonhoeffer, who lived in Tübingen. This suited Dietrich well. He loved his family and was relieved to know he would not be living among total strangers. He looked forward to the start of university.

Chapter 6

Church

Dietrich stood quietly in the circle of young men, each of whom wore a hedgehog skin on his head. It was hard for Dietrich not to laugh, but his initiation into the Igel, or Hedgehog Fraternity, was a serious matter. His father had been an Igel before him, and Dietrich looked forward to being one as well. The Igel was known as the friendliest fraternity on campus, emphasizing intellectual games and outings rather than the macho sports some of the other fraternities engaged in.

The macho sport Dietrich found the most difficult to understand was fencing. It wasn't that he thought there was anything wrong with fencing itself. But many rich, young male university students practiced the sport so they could be injured and scarred, especially on their faces. Such a scar was considered a badge of honor and was called a *renommierschmiss*. It was common to see students in class with their faces bandaged, waiting for the coveted scar to heal. Sometimes, if the wound looked like it was healing too well, a student would pack it with horsehair to inflame the wound and cause a more noticeable scar.

Dietrich's first year at Tübingen was challenging. Food rationing remained in effect, and everywhere Dietrich looked he saw young soldiers with missing limbs or eyes, a constant reminder of the price the war had cost the German people. To make matters worse, inflation was out of control in the country. Dietrich's father wrote to say that an insurance policy for one hundred thousand marks on which he had been regularly paying premiums for years had finally matured. But with the runaway inflation, all this amount of money would buy was a bottle of wine and some strawberries. And when Karl went to the store to purchase the items, he found the one hundred thousand marks would cover only the cost of a pound of strawberries. Dietrich wrote home to say that his meals were costing him one billion marks, and a little while later he wrote complaining that a loaf of bread now cost him six billion marks. Fortunately for the Bonhoeffer family, Karl Bonhoeffer saw a number of patients from around Europe who paid him in their countries' stable currencies, helping the family ride out Germany's economic woes better than most other German families.

In the middle of his first semester, Dietrich applied for permission to return briefly to Berlin for a family wedding. His older sister Ursula was marrying Rüdiger Schleicher, a promising young lawyer. Dietrich was so happy to see his family again. Even though he lived in Tübingen with his grandmother and sister Christine, he missed everyone in Berlin. At home Dietrich realized how blessed the family was to be able to afford any kind of celebration. Many German families were on the brink of ruin.

Not only did skyrocketing inflation send shock waves through the German economy, but the leaders of Germany were also concerned about the country's safety and security. One condition of the Treaty of Versailles stipulated that Germany could have an army consisting of one hundred thousand soldiers. The Russian (Soviet) army was many times that size, and Germans were concerned that if the Soviets decided to invade Germany, one hundred thousand soldiers could not stop them. In fact, many Germans doubted that one hundred thousand soldiers could even stop the rioting in the streets if it erupted again. The German government came up with a way to get around the Treaty of Versailles stipulation: as part of their coursework, male German university students received covert military training.

In November 1923 it was Dietrich's turn to undergo military training. The training would take two weeks and be overseen by the Ulm Rifle Troop. Ulm was located not far from Tübingen, and Dietrich made his way there with a number of his fellow fraternity members. When he arrived, Dietrich wrote his parents. "Today I am a soldier. Yesterday, as soon as we arrived, we were invested with a uniform and were given our equipment. Today we were given grenades and weapons. Until now, to be sure, we have done nothing but assemble and disassemble our beds."

Still, Dietrich enjoyed the physical challenge. He was now about six feet tall, had a muscular build, and liked athletics. Throughout his training he continued to write letters home.

The exercises have not been very taxing at all. There are approximately 5 hours of marching, shooting, and gymnastics daily, and 3 instruction periods, as well as other things. . . .We live 14 to a room. . . . The only thing that the examination found amiss were my eyes. I'll probably have to wear glasses when I fire a weapon. . . .

We practiced ground maneuvers with assaults and such. It is especially horrible to throw oneself down on the frozen field with a rifle and a knapsack. Tomorrow we have a big marching exercise with all our equipment, and on Wednesday we have a battalion maneuver. After that the fortnight will soon be over.

On December 1, 1923, Dietrich wrote home from Tübingen, declaring, "Dear Parents, Today I am a civilian."

Dietrich found his brief stint of army training interesting. Although he was glad to discover that he was physically fit enough to thrive under the challenge, he had no desire to be a soldier. He happily went back to his university studies.

Everything went fine until one afternoon in January 1924, when Dietrich took time off to go skating on the frozen Neckar River that ran in front of his grandmother's house. Dietrich enjoyed exercising in the bracing cold. But as he sped along on the frozen river, he lost his balance. His skates slid out from under him, and he tumbled to the ice, bumping his head hard in the process. He lapsed into unconsciousness and had to be carried back to his grandmother's house. When Dietrich didn't immediately regain consciousness, the doctor was summoned. He examined Dietrich and pronounced that there was little anyone could do except keep him warm and hope he regained consciousness soon.

Dietrich's parents were informed of the situation and quickly made their way to Tübingen. Thankfully, by the time they arrived, Dietrich was improving. However, as a psychiatrist and neurologist, Karl Bonhoeffer was concerned for his son's well-being. He examined Dietrich closely and made his diagnosis. His son had suffered a concussion, but there appeared to be no long-lasting consequences. Dietrich would make a complete recovery.

Dietrich was delighted to see his parents, and more so when they decided to stay for his eighteenth birthday on February 4. For his eighteenth birthday they gave him a special gift—an extended trip to Italy with his brother Klaus.

Dietrich was so excited he found it hard to stay in bed. His mother bought him a guidebook to Italy, and he practically memorized the whole thing, including many Italian words and phrases. He also quizzed his mother about her grandfather, the famous theologian August von Hase. Von Hase had visited Italy more than twenty times in his career and brought back several paintings that hung in the Bonhoeffer home in Berlin. Images of the Basilica of St. Peter and ancient Roman ruins flooded Dietrich's mind. It was going to be difficult to wait until the end of the school year to depart on the trip.

On April 3, 1924, Dietrich and Klaus boarded a train bound for Rome. The train was crowded with fellow Germans wanting to travel outside Germany after being isolated by the war.

Dietrich's spirits were high as the train chugged south toward Italy. As soon as it crossed the border, Dietrich quickly realized that Italy was even better than he'd imagined. The first stop was Bologna, which Dietrich found to be beautiful. Then it was on to Rome. If Bologna was beautiful, Rome was astounding. Dietrich enjoyed seeing the spectacular sites: the Colosseum and the Pantheon, the paintings of Michelangelo, and the colorful outdoor flower markets. But most of all he enjoyed his visits to the Catholic church, which surprised him, since he had been born and raised a Protestant and had not spent much time thinking about Catholicism.

From Rome, Dietrich and Klaus traveled to Naples and then caught a ferry to Sicily. Although Dietrich enjoyed everything he saw on this leg of the journey, he was eager to get back to Rome.

Once back in Rome, Dietrich set out to further investigate the Catholic church. He attended Mass at St. Peter's, where he was moved by the singing of the boys' choir. In fact, everything he experienced during the Mass deeply impressed him. While in Rome, Dietrich began attending Mass regularly. He was especially touched by the services of Holy Week. He even had an audience with the Pope, but that was not what impressed him most about the Catholic church.

Dietrich was most impressed with the idea that people from all over the world could gather under the banner of Catholicism. In Germany, he had been exposed to traditional Protestant churches, which were closely tied to the national identity of Germany and Germans. But here in Rome he was seeing all sorts of people who were able to identify with the same faith, even though they might be from countries that had fought on opposite sides during the war. In Rome, Dietrich saw people of various skin colors from far-flung cultures and nationalities who all saw themselves as belonging to one church.

Dietrich was shocked by the idea that the Christian church might be bigger than one's own country or even possibly be made up of both Protestants and Catholics. As he lay awake for many nights in Rome thinking about the concept, he recalled all the prayers and declarations by pious Christians during the war that God was on the side of the German people. Now he realized this was not true. There were Christians on both sides of the war, and God could not possibly have wanted them all to win. The more Dietrich pondered what really makes the church and what binds Christians together, even if they are of different nationalities, the more he wanted to spend time studying the notion.

Before Dietrich knew it, it was mid-June, time to return to Berlin. He hated to leave Rome. He loved being there more than almost anywhere he'd ever been. He wrote in his diary, "When I looked at St. Peter's for the last time, there was a pain in my heart, and I quickly got on the trolleycar and left."

By the time Dietrich arrived back in Berlin, he had found his life's mission—to investigate the real meaning of the word *church*.

Chapter 7

A Breath of Fresh Air

Dietrich arrived back in Berlin just in time to enroll for the summer semester at the University of Berlin. He'd always planned to spend one year at Tübingen and then switch to the University of Berlin, which had one of the best theology departments in Germany.

As he began attending classes, Dietrich had to admit it felt good living back in Berlin. Many things remained the same, but other things had changed, especially with the family. Ursula, now married, was no longer living at home. Neither was Sabine, who was studying in Breslau and had recently become engaged to a young lawyer from a Jewish background named Gerhard Liebholz. Meanwhile, Christine, who had also moved back to Berlin from Tübingen, was seeing Hans von Dohnanyi, who had just graduated with a law degree. Hans, who was two years older than Christine, lived in the Grunewald area of Berlin and was a school friend of Klaus's. Meanwhile, Dietrich's oldest brother, Karl-Friedrich, was employed at the prestigious Kaiser Wilhelm Institute, where he worked alongside Albert Einstein and Max Planck.

Even though Ursula and Sabine were gone, Dietrich found life at home as busy as ever. His mother still organized musical evenings at the house, and Dietrich was sure to be there. On Sundays he liked to get up early with his brothers and sisters and head to the Halensee station. There they would meet up with various friends for the train trip across Berlin to the Müggelsee lake area on the eastern side of town. They spent the day picnicking, talking, and walking around Müggelsee and the other lakes in the area.

The walks gave Dietrich time to think about the new ideas and concepts he was learning in his theology classes. The University of Berlin was one of the most prestigious universities in Europe, and Dietrich felt blessed to have some of the great theological thinkers of the day teaching him, men like Adolf von Harnack, Karl Holl, and Reinhold Seeberg. Surprisingly, it was not the writings or teachings of any of these three that Dietrich felt most drawn to. Dietrich was drawn to the work of a professor at Göttingen University, 150 miles away. This man, Karl Barth, was not even German, but was Swiss. What was important to Dietrich was not Barth's nationality but the radical ideas he put forward. Barth redirected scholarly theology back to the Bible and away from the liberal thought that was pervasive at the time. He declared that God was transcendent and unknowable by man except through revelation, and that revelation could be discerned through studying the Bible.

Dietrich found Barth's view to be a breath of fresh air. It provided him a different framework from which to approach the Bible. It was at odds with what he was learning from Adolf von Harnack, who asserted that man couldn't speculate about the existence of God—it is unknowable. According to Harnack's approach, all one could do was draw lessons and conclusions from the biblical texts and their history with the aid of science and logic.

Dietrich was also both astonished and delighted to learn that his cousin, Hans-Christoph von Hase, who had gone to Göttingen University to study physics, had been so impressed with a lecture by Karl Barth that he had switched to studying theology. Now there would be two theologians in the family, and someone for Dietrich to have deep conversations with.

By the end of his first year at the University of Berlin, Dietrich had decided on his thesis topic. Drawing from his experience in Rome the year before, Dietrich wanted to study the true meaning of the church. In particular, he wanted to explore the notion that it was more than a historic organization or current institution. He titled his thesis *Sanctorum Communio (The Communion of Saints): A Dogmatic Inquiry Into the Sociology of the Church.*

Around the time Dietrich finalized the subject of his thesis, he attended the wedding of his older sister

Christine, who married Hans von Dohnanyi. Now one less sibling was living at home. However, Grandmother Bonhoeffer soon took Christine's place. She was getting older, her house in Tübingen had become too big for her to care for, and she moved to Berlin to live with the family.

During his second year at the University of Berlin, Dietrich embarked on another adventure. Part of his degree requirement stipulated that he find a way to serve in a local church. Dietrich began attending the Grunewald Lutheran Church regularly, something new to him. He asked his mother, herself a devout Christian, why she had never insisted that he or his siblings attend church. Paula's answer was simple. Her father had been a pastor, and she had grown up in the church and been a Sunday school teacher herself. In the process, she saw some church adults push strange and frightening ideas onto young children at Sunday school, and she decided not to let that happen to her children. Instead she taught them Bible lessons and read them stories at home. Dietrich was satisfied with her answer. He had no doubt he'd received a genuine Christian upbringing from her.

Following in his mother's footsteps, Dietrich decided to take on the challenge of teaching Sunday school in the parish church. At first he was unsure whether he would enjoy such work and, more important, whether the children would enjoy being around him. Dietrich need not have worried. He soon discovered he had a natural gift for working with and teaching children. He loved planning lessons that would help even the youngest children understand ideas about God, and he often made up parables and fairy tales to make his points. The children loved Dietrich's approach, and soon his Sunday school class was overflowing with enthusiastic children. In fact, the class grew so big that he enlisted the help of his sister Susanne to take the overflow. Together they formed a strong team.

On April 6, 1926, Dietrich, along with the rest of the Bonhoeffer family, attended Sabine's wedding. Dietrich's twenty-year-old twin sister married Gerhard Liebholz, who at twenty-eight years of age was already a full professor of law at the University of Greifswald. Now all of the Bonhoeffer girls except Susanne were married. Ursula and her husband, Rüdiger, had children, making Dietrich an uncle and his parents grandparents. Dietrich smiled as he saw how much his parents savored their new role.

Dietrich enjoyed teaching children so much that in April 1927 he started another group, the Thursday Circle, and cast a wider net than the church group. In fact, many of the teenage boys whom he invited to his house for the gathering were Jewish. The Thursday Circle covered a range of topics. One week Dietrich might lead a conversation on the gods of the ancient Germans and the next week an exploration of the Muslim faith. The Thursday Circle often met for outings on Saturdays as well, attending operas, ballets, and guest lectures at the university. Dietrich's involvement in the group brought him a great deal of satisfaction. He believed Germany needed strong, intelligent young men to help rebuild the country and strengthen its fledgling democracy.

The situation in Germany had improved. The runaway inflation of the German mark had been stabilized, and things remained calm in the streets. Even so, many small political parties, particularly right-wing groups, were vying for power in the country. Dietrich was too busy to keep up with all the political maneuvering going on, and the subject was rarely brought up at home. Science and music and family occupied conversation in the Bonhoeffer home.

Life continued at a brisk pace for Dietrich, who was eager to complete his theological studies and so took on many extra classes. At the same time, he continued to teach Sunday school, run the Thursday Circle with its Saturday outings, and play an active role in the life of his family. The Saturday evening musical gatherings his mother hosted were attended by friends, neighbors, and relatives, including an ever-growing number of grandchildren. Despite his other responsibilities, Dietrich attended each musical gathering, playing the piano as he still loved to do and entertaining his young nieces and nephews.

By now, Dietrich had a girlfriend, a fellow theology student named Elizabeth Zinn. Elizabeth shared Dietrich's enthusiasm for the ideas of Karl Barth, and the two of them enjoyed long conversations as they toured the museums of Berlin and attended the symphony.

Dietrich's time at the University of Berlin passed quickly. Before he knew it, 1927 was drawing to a close. Dietrich had finished his thesis and successfully defended it. He graduated summa cum laude, the only person in his class to receive the distinction. At twenty-one years of age, he was now Dr. Dietrich Bonhoeffer.

Dietrich's life was at a crossroads. He could move in either of two directions: he could become a university lecturer and pursue further theological studies, or he could become a pastor and help shape the life of the church he had studied so much about.

Dietrich's family assumed he would choose teaching at university level, but Dietrich's heart pulled him in the other direction. Two days after Christmas 1927, Dietrich received a telephone call from Lutheran Superintendent Max Diestel, who offered him a yearlong position as an assistant pastor at a German-speaking church in Barcelona, Spain. Somehow Dietrich felt a year in another country serving the German population there would be good for him. His parents were shocked when they heard the news. They'd hoped that if Dietrich did take on a pastoral role outside Germany it would be in London or Paris or Rome, not in a place like Barcelona. Still, the more Dietrich thought about going to Barcelona as an assistant pastor, the more he liked the idea. He decided that one year away from everything and everyone he knew would be a great test of his faith and manhood.

Four days after his twenty-second birthday, Dietrich boarded a train in Berlin and headed westward to Paris. From there he took another train south to Barcelona. As the train rolled along, Dietrich was nervous. Going to Barcelona had seemed like a good idea, but now here he was, headed nearly a thousand miles from Berlin to another country, to work under a pastor he had never met.

As the train pulled into Paris, the city was enveloped in damp mist. Soon Dietrich was on his way again, headed south to Barcelona, and the sun came out as he left Paris behind. Dietrich watched as the train skirted the Mediterranean coast, passing quaint fishing villages on the left and mile after mile of almond groves on the right, until it reached Barcelona.

Pastor Fritz Olbricht was waiting at the train station. He was an older man and looked tired. He shook Dietrich's hand warmly and explained that he was about to head back to Germany for a three-month vacation.

Pastor Olbricht found Dietrich a room in a boarding house near the church. It was run by three Spanish women who welcomed Dietrich warmly. Three other German men rented rooms in the boarding house, and they were friendly toward Dietrich too.

Until this point in his life, Dietrich had not thought much about why Germans would choose to live in a foreign country. He soon learned they did it for all sorts of reasons: some were seeking adventure or were involved in international businesses, while others were fleeing the law. He described his findings in a letter to his family.

One has to deal with the strangest persons, with whom one would otherwise scarcely have exchanged a word: bums, vagabonds, criminals on the run, many foreign legionaries, lion and other animal trainers who have

run away from the Krone Circus on its Spanish tour, German dancers from the music-halls
here, German murderers on the run. . . .

Dietrich came in contact with all these people in
the course of his duties. As assistant pastor he con-
ducted services in Barcelona and other smaller towns
and at the sailors' mission. The church ran a welfare
office where Germans could come if they were in
trouble. Many of those who came to the office came
seeking financial help to return to Germany.

Approximately six thousand Germans were living in Barcelona, and about forty of them came to
church regularly. Since the church had no Sunday
school, Dietrich decided to start one. Things did not
begin well. Only one girl showed up the first Sunday,
but Dietrich was not deterred. He taught the full Sunday school lesson to the single student, and the next
week fifteen children showed up ready to learn. By
the end of the first month, forty children were regularly attending Sunday school.

Dietrich had opportunity to visit the families of
these children, and he was soon encouraging the parents to come along to church. This proved a successful strategy and led to Dietrich's decision to become
more involved in Barcelona's German community.
Dietrich joined the chorale society, where he was
quickly appointed to play the piano; the German
society, where he liked to play chess; and the tennis
club. Dietrich attended these three groups regularly,
but his main focus was drawing people to church. He
loved writing and delivering sermons each Sunday

and soon struck on the idea of a series of lectures that might interest a wider audience. During the winter he gave a series of four lectures open to the general public. Large numbers of people attended, and Dietrich was soon widely recognized around Barcelona.

At Easter, Klaus came to visit his younger brother. By now Dietrich was fluent in Spanish and was delighted to show Klaus the sights of Barcelona, including his favorite Saturday activity—the bullfight. Something about the power and rage of the bulls, along with the skill and courage of the matadors, thrilled Dietrich to the core. When he wrote to his sister Sabine about his enthusiasm for the sport, she could not believe he found it so compelling. "I would not have such a spectacle on a silver platter," she indignantly wrote back.

Despite his sister's objections, Dietrich went to bullfights as often as possible, and when his parents visited him later in the year, he took them along.

Before Dietrich knew it, his year as an assistant pastor in Barcelona was up. The German congregation asked him to stay on permanently at the church, but Dietrich decided against it. Although he had loved his sojourn in Barcelona, he felt it was time to head back to Berlin and take up a new challenge. Exactly what that challenge was, he didn't know, but he welcomed the invitation to live back with his family in Berlin.

Chapter 8

New York

Dietrich arrived back in Berlin eleven days after his twenty-third birthday. His time in Barcelona had convinced him that he could not settle for a life either as a university lecturer or as a pastor—he wanted to do both. As a result, Dietrich returned to the university to complete a second thesis, the requirement to become a lecturer.

Dietrich slipped back easily into studying and family activities. While he had never been particularly interested in politics, he noticed some changes that had taken place during the year he had been gone. Germany seemed to be moving away from economic disaster. The United States was pouring millions of dollars in loans into Germany, and Foreign Minister Gustav Stresemann had negotiated with the

Allies for a reduction in the amount of war reparations and for the Rhineland to be returned to German
control by June 1930, five years ahead of schedule.

Dietrich saw these as hopeful signs, but he also
detected some troubling trends. The Weimar Republic was still lurching along. In 1929 the government
consisted of five main parties: the Social Democratic
Party with 153 seats, the Catholic Center Party with 78
seats, the National Party with 73 seats, the Communist
Party with 54 seats, and the National Socialist German
Workers' Party (or Nazi Party) with 12 seats. Many
other smaller parties held a combined 121 seats among
them. With so many parties, it was nearly impossible
to get anything done in the Reichstag or parliament.
The German people were frustrated that no one party
had enough power to get the economy moving prop-
erly. Because of this, many Germans longed to have
the Kaiser back—one man with the power to bring
everyone into line. Yet they knew the Allies would
never allow the Kaiser to return to Germany from
exile in Holland. Somehow they would have to find a
new way to become a proud nation once again.

During 1929, Dietrich attended the wedding of
his younger sister Susanne. It was a happy day for
him. Not only was his sister getting married, but she
was also marrying Walter Dress, a fellow theology
student at the University of Berlin whom Dietrich
had introduced to the family.

Nine months after Dietrich returned from Barcelona, two events occurred in Germany that drew his
attention. The first was the death of Foreign Minister

Stresemann, who died of a stroke. With him died the hope of many for a strong, peaceful Germany to once again take her place as a leader in Europe. The government was still reeling from Stresemann's death when another disaster struck. On Tuesday, October 29, 1929, the stock market in the United States crashed. As the value of the market sank, its fall echoed around the world, especially in Germany, where most of the money used to stimulate the economy had been borrowed from the United States. Now, suddenly those American banks wanted their money back, and quickly. Loans were called in, German banks closed their doors, men were laid off from their jobs, and the arguments between the right-wing Nazis and the left-wing communists inside and outside the government reached a boiling point. Riots took place in the streets of Berlin, with police killing protesters. Dietrich realized he could no longer stand on the sidelines and watch the political situation unfold. He wasn't sure what he could do, but a feeling of dread overcame him when he tried to imagine a bright future for his country.

In early 1930, as Dietrich continued his theological studies and pondered the political situation in Germany, he attended Karl-Friedrich's wedding. Karl-Friedrich married Grete von Dohnanyi, younger sister of Christine's husband, Hans von Dohnanyi. By now Karl-Friedrich's reputation as a world-renowned scientist was well established.

Despite the economic depression that settled over Germany, many German students continued studying abroad, particularly in the United States. The German Academic Exchange Service offered to pay a student's passage to the United States, and various American colleges offered scholarships.

Dietrich didn't feel particularly drawn to study in the United States. He would have preferred studying in England or India. However, Superintendent Max Diestel told him about an opportunity to go to the United States and study at Union Theological Seminary in New York City on a Sloane Fellowship. That July, Dietrich had completed his second thesis, titled *Act and Being*, and at age twenty-four he was a year from being ordained a pastor. Diestel encouraged him to study in the United States to pass the time until ordination. Dietrich followed the superintendent's advice and applied for the fellowship at Union Theological Seminary. He was quickly accepted to the seminary and immediately booked passage to New York aboard the liner *Columbus*, departing from Bremerhaven on September 6, 1930.

Things were happening so fast that Dietrich barely had time to keep his family updated. Karl-Friedrich, who had just returned from a lecture tour of the United States, told him what to expect when he got to America. Then, on September 4, Dietrich attended his brother Klaus's wedding to Emmi Delbrück. Now all six of Dietrich's brothers and sisters were married. He was the only one who was single, and his sisters teased him about it. Dietrich continued to see Elizabeth Zinn, though they both felt free to pursue their own interests and did not speak of marriage.

The day after Klaus's wedding, Dietrich set out for Bremerhaven on the Baltic Sea. As he crossed Germany on his way to the port, the country was in an uproar. Six million people were now unemployed, the most since the war. For many people, the Nazi Party, with its strong appeal to German nationalist sentiment, seemed the best hope for the country. Dietrich didn't know what to make of it all, but he hoped the upcoming election for seats in the Reichstag on September 14 would help clarify things.

The next day in Bremerhaven, Dietrich boarded the *Columbus*. The vessel represented a new beginning for Germany after the war. At the end of the fighting, the Allies had taken all of Germany's great oceangoing liners as partial payment of war reparations. The *Columbus*, built in 1922, was Germany's first postwar ocean liner. She carried 1,650 passengers and was one of the first liners to have an outside swimming pool installed on her top deck as well as a platform for nighttime dancing. Dietrich was shown to his cabin and after stowing his luggage, he went up on deck for the departure. Once they were steaming along the Baltic Sea, Dietrich went to the salon to write to his grandmother.

> My cabin seems not unfavorably located. It lies deep in the belly of the ship. I actually haven't seen my cabin companion yet. I've tried to get a picture of him from the items he has left about. The hat, the walking cane, and a novel . . . suggest an educated young American to

me. . . . I have eaten two enormous meals with a healthy appetite; in a word, I'm enjoying the ship as long as it can be enjoyed. I've also gotten to know several nice people, so the time is going by quickly. I'll soon be going to bed since I'd like to see as much of England as possible early tomorrow morning. Just now we are traveling along the Belgian coast. You can see lights way off in the distance.

After Dietrich had finished his letter to his grandmother, he wandered out on deck. The ship was impressive, especially the large swimming pool. He planned to swim in it every day as a way to stay fit while on board.

When he returned to his cabin, Dietrich met his cabinmate for the voyage. Just as he speculated, he was an American. Dr. Edmund De Long Lucas was the principal of Forman Christian College in Lahore, India. He was returning to the United States to raise money for the college. As they talked, Dietrich knew the two of them would become good friends, especially when he learned that Dr. Lucas had earned his doctorate at Columbia University, right across the street from Union Theological Seminary. Dietrich peppered his cabinmate with all sorts of questions about life in New York.

That night Dietrich slept soundly and in the morning was up on deck watching the south coast of England slip by. He wished he had time to visit the place but promised himself he would come back to England one day. In the meantime, Dietrich was determined to enjoy his six days on board the *Columbus*. He met someone else who was eager to explore the ship, eleven-year-old Richard Ern. Richard and his mother were returning from a visit to Switzerland.

The voyage across the North Atlantic passed quickly, and before he knew it, Dietrich was standing on deck watching the Statue of Liberty as the *Columbus* slipped into New York Harbor. His young friend Richard eagerly pointed out the recently completed Chrysler Building gleaming in the sun. He proudly informed Dietrich that it was the tallest building on the planet.

At mid-afternoon on Friday, the *Columbus* docked and Dietrich was free to disembark. Waiting for him on the dock were his distant cousins, Harold and Irma Boericke, who lived about sixty miles away in Philadelphia. Dietrich exchanged greetings with the Boerickes, loaded his luggage into the back of their car, and set off with them for Philadelphia, passing through the Holland Tunnel under the Hudson River. Dietrich was intrigued with the countryside. The road they traveled along was clogged with cars, and everyone seemed to be going somewhere in a hurry.

Waiting at the house in Philadelphia were the three Boericke children: Ray, Betty, and Binkie. Dietrich spent a delightful week with his American relatives before they drove him back to New York City to begin fall semester at Union Theological Seminary. Dietrich didn't know what his role would be. He wasn't enrolled as a degree-seeking student or as a lecturer, though he could have been either. Instead he chose to audit classes, which meant he had a lot of freedom to study and go where he pleased.

When he got back to New York, Dietrich learned the results of the Reichstag elections that had been held in Germany on September 14. The results surprised and perplexed him. The Nazis had gone from holding twelve seats in the Reichstag to holding 107 seats. They had gained ninety-five seats in the election, making them the second-largest party in the Reichstag. By contrast, the Communist Party gained only twenty-three seats, and the Social Democratic Party, the largest party in the Reichstag, lost ten seats. Many Germans seemed to breathe a sigh of relief at the result. To them it seemed that at long last one party was becoming strong enough to lead Germany into a new era of respect and power. Dietrich was not one of them. To him and the other members of the Bonhoeffer family, the Nazis and their leader Adolf Hitler were extremists.

Dietrich started classes at the seminary, and it took him only a few days to decide he'd made the right choice to audit classes. As much as he tried to look on the bright side, he was appalled by the different way the seminary went about teaching its students. Dietrich had come from one of the most rigorous systems of teaching in the world. Now he found himself surrounded by people who did not seem to care about the great strands of European theology. These people even laughed at the teachings of Martin Luther and asked Dietrich what someone as far back in time as Luther had to do with anything today.

In a letter home to Max Diestel, Dietrich wrote, "There is no theology here. . . . The students—on average twenty-five to thirty years old—are completely clueless with respect to what dogmatics is really about. They are unfamiliar with even the most basic questions."

It was not a promising start, but Dietrich soon found a few friends with whom he could have meaningful conversations. They were an unusual group: Erwin Sutz, a Swiss; Jean Lasserre, a Frenchman; and Frank Fisher, an African-American man from Alabama. Dietrich loved the different perspectives these men brought to their conversations, and it wasn't long before Frank invited Dietrich to attend a service at the Abyssinian Baptist Church in nearby Harlem.

Dietrich wasn't sure what to expect as he headed to the church on 138th Street. What he found astonished him: the church building was large and imposing. When Frank explained how the building had been financed, Dietrich was amazed. The church had begun in 1808 when a group of Africans and Ethiopian sea merchants left First Baptist Church in lower Manhattan. The people refused to accept the racially segregated seating that took place there and left to form their own church. Drawing on the ancient name of Ethiopia—Abyssinia—they founded the Abyssinian Baptist Church. They believed that even if there was racism outside the church, inside the church all people should be treated equally as Christian brothers and sisters, and that's what they strove for. Over the years the Abyssinian Baptist Church outgrew several facilities until the large church on 138th Street was built. The building was completely financed by tithes from the congregation.

Dietrich was impressed and sat transfixed as the pastor, Dr. Adam Clayton Powell, Sr., preached. Dr. Powell was the liveliest pastor he'd ever heard. Dietrich soon found himself casting off his German reserve, singing and swaying along with the throng of people in attendance. Frank explained that the Abyssinian Baptist Church had a membership of nearly fourteen thousand, making it the largest Protestant church in the United States.

Attending the Abyssinian Baptist Church in Harlem was a life-changing experience for Dietrich. He asked Frank about race relations in the United States and why black people were treated differently than whites. Frank invited Dietrich to go to Washington, DC, with him for Thanksgiving. Dietrich readily agreed, and he and Frank and another African-American student drove to Washington. When they stopped on the way for lunch, Dietrich was shocked when the waiter said they would have to leave. Black people were not welcome to sit with whites. Having grown up in Europe, where everyone was pretty much of one race, Dietrich found it impossible to fathom why people refused to get to know each other simply because of skin color. Things only got worse when they arrived in Washington and Frank took Dietrich sightseeing. It was illegal for them to be in the same tram or sit together on the bus. Dietrich could hardly believe that this was America in 1930.

Knowing that his brother had also been to the United States, Dietrich wrote to Karl-Friedrich saying, "I want to have a look at church conditions in the South, which allegedly can still be quite peculiar, and get to know the situation of the Negroes in a bit more detail."

The letter he received back from his brother surprised Dietrich. Karl-Friedrich explained that he'd been offered a university post in the United States but had chosen not to accept it, because he didn't want to raise his children in a racially divided country. Dietrich knew exactly what his brother meant.

After returning to New York, Dietrich committed himself to work at the Abyssinian Baptist Church. He knew he looked very blond and pale compared to the other church members, but he figured that if he made himself useful they would accept him, and they did. Soon Dietrich was a well-loved figure at the church as he attended Sunday services regularly and taught a Sunday school class.

Dietrich's next experience had nothing to do with church or religion, but it challenged his thinking nonetheless. It occurred when he agreed to accompany Jean Lasserre, his French friend at Union Theological Seminary, to see a newly released movie called *All Quiet on the Western Front*. The movie, based on the best-selling novel of the same name by Erich Maria Remarque, was about young German soldiers during the war.

Within minutes of sitting down in the movie theater, Dietrich was unsure whether he should have come. The movie opened with a group of enthusiastic young German schoolboys being lectured on the joys of serving the Fatherland as soldiers. At first the boys were reluctant to embrace the message, but as the teacher persisted, they caught a vision of the glorious war that awaited them. In a fit of patriotic fervor they left the classroom to sign up to fight.

Watching the action on screen, Dietrich cast his mind back to that time. He had been eight years old when war was declared. He remembered his exuberance and how his mother had chided his sister for being overly excited. He remembered Fräulein Lenchen and how she talked about the young heroes dying. But most of all, he remembered his brother Walter. As he watched, Dietrich wondered whether the movie echoed Walter's experience—excitement and discipline followed by despair and death. He remembered Walter's body being returned home in a coffin and how his mother was never the same.

The movie screen flickered as black and white images of gunfire and bombs, blood and barbed wire, told the unfolding story of the boys. Toward the end of the movie, one of the German boys became stuck in a bombed-out hollow with a dying French soldier who was also young, confused, and scared. As Dietrich watched the final minutes of the movie, he wiped away tears that flowed down his cheeks. He looked over and saw that Jean was also crying silently. The American audience had a different reaction, cheering when the movie ended. Dietrich and Jean quietly made their way outside.

Back in his dorm room at the seminary, Dietrich sobbed. It all seemed too much. The senselessness of war and what it had cost his family and his country overcame him. Later he talked to Jean about the movie. Jean was a pacifist who opposed war under any circumstance. Dietrich understood his friend's position, though he did not quite go that far himself. Nonetheless, *All Quiet on the Western Front* had thoroughly shaken his notion of war being a noble venture.

As Christmas approached, Dietrich wondered what to do. He had spent Thanksgiving in Washington and was eager for a new experience. In the end he settled on a trip to Cuba to visit his childhood teacher, Käthe Horn, who was teaching at a German school in Havana. Getting to Cuba was an adventure in itself. Dietrich and Erwin Sutz, his Swiss friend, took a train south to Miami, Florida, then caught another train to Key West. This stretch of track, known as the Overseas Railroad, was spectacular as the train traveled over long bridges above the open sea. Dietrich sat by the window watching in wonder as they crossed the sea and dozens of tiny islands, or keys, some just a few feet above sea level. In Key West they boarded a ferry for the ninety-mile voyage south to Havana.

The noise and hubbub of Havana reminded Dietrich of his time in Barcelona. Since Spanish was Cuba's national language, Dietrich was able to pick up with the Spanish he had learned while living in Spain. He loved the sun and warm temperatures in Cuba. Snow had already been on the ground in New York when he and Erwin had left to head south. Käthe showed Dietrich and Erwin the sights and sounds of Havana. Cuba turned out to be a different and exciting place full of history, culture, and music. On Christmas Day, Dietrich preached the sermon to the German congregation in Havana.

On the way back to New York, Dietrich made some detours to see more of the South and observe how African-Americans were treated there. He was not impressed with what he saw. From his first visit to the Abyssinian Baptist Church, though, Dietrich had fallen in love with Negro spiritual music, and as he traveled the South, he bought as many records of Negro spirituals as he could find.

When the academic year came to a close at Union Theological Seminary in May 1931, Dietrich and Jean took a road trip all the way to Mexico. Dietrich was interested in seeing firsthand the Mexican form of Catholicism, and in Mexico the two men visited many churches and cathedrals before making their way back north to New York.

Dietrich and Jean arrived in New York on June 17. After ten months packed full of activity in the United States, it was time for Dietrich to return to Germany. Dietrich set sail from New York on June 20, 1931.

As he made his way home, Dietrich felt like a different person. For the first time in his life, he had lived completely outside of a German environment. He understood the way the Allies viewed Germans, and he'd had some surprises of his own. He could not understand how a country like the United States could talk so much about justice and liberty for all while at the same time allowing racial discrimination. He was glad to be returning to a country where people of different ethnicities were treated equally, or so he thought. What Dietrich didn't know was how much Germany had changed in the short time he'd been away.

Chapter 9

Dark Developments

Dietrich was glad to be home in Berlin. His parents welcomed him warmly. It was good to see his siblings again and their ever-growing brood of children. Yet Dietrich was amazed at how much Germany had changed. Now that the Nazis were the second-largest political party in the country, they were trying to exert their influence in every area of culture. Dietrich wrote to his Swiss friend Erwin Sutz, "The outlook is really exceptionally grim. We are standing at a tremendous turning point in world history."

Soon after arriving back in Germany, Dietrich visited Karl Barth in Bonn. Given the impact Barth's theology and writings had had on him, Dietrich was eager to meet the man. The two of them spent many hours together discussing their points of view, and

Dietrich came away from the meeting more impressed with Barth than he had imagined he would.

In Berlin, Dietrich became a lecturer at the University of Berlin. Although his subject was theology, he liked to challenge his students. One of his lectures was on the subject of whether the church is outdated. "Nowadays we often ask ourselves whether we still need the church, whether we still need God. But this is the wrong question to be asking. We are the ones who are being questioned. The church exists, and God exists, and we are asked whether we are willing to be a part of the church and of service, for God needs us," he declared.

Dietrich was speaking to himself as much as to his students. He loved being a theology lecturer, but he was also sure God had called him to be a pastor. In fact, he was ordained a pastor on November 15, 1931, and began looking for pastoral opportunities. It wasn't long before he was asked to take over the confirmation class of fifty boys at Zionskirche, in the suburb of Wedding, a notoriously rough and poverty-stricken area in the north of Berlin.

In Germany, parents sent their children to confirmation class not because they felt it was good for their children but because it was the law. This meant that confirmation classes were often filled with unruly boys who did not care about religion at all, and the boys' class at Zionskirche in Wedding was no exception, as Dietrich soon found out.

As Dietrich and the local pastor walked upstairs to the third floor where the confirmation class was held, the fourteen- and fifteen-year-old boys who made up the class peered over the banister yelling and hurling garbage down on Dietrich and the pastor. Dietrich's heart sank. This was not going to be an easy assignment. In the third-floor classroom the pastor introduced Dietrich to the boys as their new catechism teacher. Immediately the boys began chanting the first syllable of his name, "Bon! Bon! Bon!" The pastor shrugged in despair and left Dietrich alone at the front of the class. Dietrich stood silently, his hands in his pockets, and waited for the chanting to subside. As the minutes passed and he failed to respond to the taunting, the boys began to tire and quiet down. When the chant stopped, Dietrich spoke in a soft voice, telling the boys about his experiences in Harlem and the Abyssinian Baptist Church. At first only the boys in the front row could hear, but soon the room was completely quiet as those at the back strained to hear. Dietrich promised to tell the boys more about Harlem next time. At the next confirmation class the boys stayed quiet and listened as Dietrich described his American travels and told several Bible stories. From then on Dietrich had few discipline problems with the class.

Now that he had control of the unruly class, Dietrich wanted to invest more than just an hour a week in the boys. He rented a room in the neighborhood and moved in. His room was above a bakery, and Dietrich gave the baker instructions that if any of the boys showed up to see him, they should be allowed up to his room, even if he was not there. He also let the boys know his new address and that his door was always unlocked and open for anyone who wanted to visit.

Before long, boys started showing up at Dietrich's room in the evenings. Dietrich taught them chess, and as they played, Dietrich talked to the boys, learning more about them while trying to reinforce what he was teaching in the confirmation class. In no time at all, Dietrich had won both the boys' friendship and their respect.

Confirmation day for the boys was to be held March 13, 1932, the same day as Germany's presidential election. The German president held a lot of power, and Paul von Hindenburg had served in the post for seven years. At eighty-four years of age and in poor health, Hindenburg wanted to step down but was persuaded to put himself up for reelection when the Nazi Party leader, Adolf Hitler, entered the presidential race.

. As an Austrian rather than a German citizen, Hitler should have been ineligible to run for president. He had also been tried and convicted of treason for his role in a failed attempt to overthrow the government in November 1923. He spent a year in prison, where he passed the time writing a rambling book about his life and beliefs, titled *Mein Kampf*, "My Struggle." But in the days leading up to the presidential election, Hitler found a loophole that allowed him to become a German citizen and run in the election. To stop Adolf Hitler from attaining the post, Hindenburg ran again.

As confirmation day in Wedding and election day in Germany approached, Berlin's streets were filled with Nazi Party members riding around on the backs of trucks with megaphones in hand, trying to stir up support for Adolf Hitler.

On Sunday, March 13, Dietrich was at Zionskirche in Wedding, delivering the confirmation sermon. It was normal in such a sermon to deliver a stern warning to the boys, but given all that was happening in Germany that day, Dietrich decided not to be hard on the boys. Instead he told them, "Today I must not make your prospect for the future seem harder and darker than it already is—and I know that many of you know a great many of the hard facts of life. Today you are not to be given fear of life but courage. And so today in the church we shall speak more than ever of hope, the hope that we have and which no one can take from you."

In the presidential election, Hindenburg eventually won 53 percent of the votes, while Hitler received 36 percent. Dietrich breathed a sigh of relief. Yet he was greatly concerned about Hitler. Gaining 36 percent of the votes cast for president gave Hitler a lot of power, even if he wasn't president.

The Bonhoeffer family waited and watched as German parliamentary elections were held on July 31, 1932. When the results were announced, the Nazi Party had won nearly 38 percent of the votes and 230 seats in the Reichstag. However, it was not enough for them to rule Germany outright. In the weeks following, despite intense negotiations, it became clear that none of the other parties wanted to enter into a coalition with the Nazis, and a political stalemate ensued. As a result, a second parliamentary election was called for November 6.

Dietrich was deeply concerned. Something sinister seemed to be happening in Germany. Dietrich wasn't exactly sure what it was, but he felt the need to alert Germans to the dangers ahead for the nation. An opportunity to do this came when he was asked to speak at the Kaiser Wilhelm Memorial Church, Berlin's beautiful cathedral, on Reformation Sunday, the same day as the election: November 6, 1932. On Reformation Sunday, German Protestants celebrated their hero, Martin Luther, who had led the Reformation.

As Dietrich made his way to the church to deliver his sermon, the streets were again filled with Nazi Party members riding on the backs of trucks with their megaphones. As Dietrich stood to deliver his Reformation Day sermon, his words quickly cut through any thought of celebration. He told the congregation they had strayed far from Luther and that it was time for them to live by their convictions, just as Luther had stood by his convictions when he nailed his ninety-five theses to the church door in Wittenberg in 1517.

The sermon was not popular. People had come to church that day to feel good about themselves and their heritage. They left feeling confused and angry with Dietrich. But he didn't care. Something told him tough times were ahead and people needed to take a serious look at the changes happening in their country.

Later that day Dietrich learned the results of the parliamentary elections. They were no more conclusive than those of the July election. The Nazis had won 33 percent of the votes, or 196 seats in the Reichstag; the Social Democratic Party, 121 seats; the Communist Party, 100 seats; the Catholic Center Party, 90 seats; and the Nationalist Party, 52 seats. A range of other small parties held 32 seats among them. The Nazis had lost 34 seats from the July election, while the Communists had gained 11. Although Dietrich was pleased that the Nazis had lost seats in the latest election, still no single party had enough seats to form a government.

The weeks that followed were filled with political wrangling and rancor, but eventually Hitler and the Nazi Party wore down President Hindenburg. In an attempt to overcome the political impasse in the country, on January 30, 1933, Hindenburg appointed Hitler chancellor of a coalition government. Without the majority's vote, an Austrian criminal had become the most powerful man in Germany. Few Germans worried too much about this. They were just glad that Germany once again had a strong and vital leader. They hoped he would show the rest of Europe that Germans were strong and brave and would no longer be bullied by other countries as they had been in the Treaty of Versailles.

Now that Hitler was chancellor, the entire Bonhoeffer family held their breath and waited to see what would happen next. Twenty-eight days later they found out. On February 27, 1933, the Reichstag, the German parliament building, went up in flames. Nervously Dietrich watched the fire from the second-story window of his parents' house, certain that Hitler and the Nazis would turn the incident to their advantage.

The next day the newspapers in Berlin carried the headline that a Dutch communist by the name of Marinus van der Lubbe had been found in the burned-out building. Van der Lubbe was accused of setting the fire. Instead of treating the incident as arson and allowing the German justice system to deal with the situation, the Nazi Party treated the fire as a matter of national security. Hitler whipped the German people into a frenzy of hatred toward foreigners and communists alike. Joseph Goebbels, the Nazi propaganda minister, proclaimed, "This is the beginning of the Communist Revolution! We must not wait a minute. We will show no mercy. Every Communist official must be shot where he is found. Every Communist deputy must be this very night strung up."

On February 28, Hitler responded to the situation with the Reichstag Fire Decree. He claimed that a secret investigation had uncovered a plot by the communists to pillage and burn Berlin to the ground, murder anticommunists, and create civil war in Germany. The burning of the parliament building, Hitler said, was the first stage in this campaign of terror against the German people. Hitler then proposed a perfectly simple solution: he and the Nazi Party would take care of everything and keep everyone safe. All the German people had to do was give them the power to make decisions for them and the good of Germany. To many Germans this seemed like a great idea. They would be safe and secure, led by a strong man with a loyal party to back him up. Peace and prosperity would surely follow.

President Hindenburg quickly signed the Reichstag Fire Decree into law. The decree suspended most of the civil liberties in Germany as set forth in the Weimar Constitution. This meant that German people could not expect any privacy. Their phone calls could be tapped, their letters read, their houses searched, and their children questioned—and they had no right to protest. It also meant an end to certain freedoms. German newspapers could print only things the Nazi Party approved of. People could not assemble in groups without approval or talk about anything that was anti-Hitler or against the Nazi Party. The decree also stripped away the right of states within Germany to make their own laws—all laws now came from the Reich government and were to be obeyed without question.

Dietrich and his family were shocked at the speed at which things were changing. The Nazis were right-wing extremists using emotionalism and nationalistic slogans to stir up the people. They also knew how to manipulate the German political system to their advantage, evidenced by the way they got the Enabling Act passed in the Reichstag on March 23, 1933. To pass, this act needed two-thirds of the

Reichstag members to vote for it, and the Nazis had nowhere near the number of seats needed for that kind of majority. However, the Reichstag Fire Decree allowed the Nazis to eliminate from contention the communists, who held one hundred seats. Through intimidation, threats, thuggery, and intense negotiation, the Nazis managed to get enough votes to pass the Enabling Act into law.

The Enabling Act was so named because it enabled the chancellor and his cabinet to enact laws in Germany without the participation of the Reichstag. In short, Hitler and his fellow Nazis could now pass laws without any parliamentary consent or control. In certain circumstances those laws could deviate from the constitution. Any thought of cooperation or coalition in government had been swept away. The German people wanted to feel safe and proud again, and Adolf Hitler now had the power to do that for them. The Third Reich had begun.

Dietrich did not trust the Nazis, and it took only two weeks for him to learn that Adolf Hitler had darker plans for Germany than anyone could have imagined.

Chapter 10

Segregation

In the second-floor bedroom of his parents' house, Dietrich sat quietly, though his mind was in turmoil. He found it hard to take in what was happening in Germany. Adolf Hitler had instigated a policy he called *Gleichschaltung* (synchronization), which was meant to bring the entire order of German life into line with Nazi Party values. One piece of this reordering in particular stunned Dietrich. It was known as the Aryan Paragraph, and it would take effect on April 7, 1933. The Aryan Paragraph stated that in the interest of restoring order to Germany's Civil Service, all government jobs must be held by people of Aryan or European heritage. Those people of Jewish heritage, even Jews who had converted to Christianity or been raised as Christians, were to have their jobs terminated immediately. Hitler had made it clear that he expected German churches to follow the same approach outlined in the Aryan Paragraph.

Dietrich thought of his good friend and fellow theology student Franz Hildebrandt, who was now a pastor at Kleinmachnow. Franz's mother was of Jewish descent, which meant that Franz would be affected by the introduction of the Aryan Paragraph. And what about his own brother-in-law, Gerhard Leibholz? Gerhard was a successful law professor at Göttingen University and had converted from Judaism to Christianity. What would the Aryan Paragraph mean for him?

As he thought about what the Aryan Paragraph meant for Germany and in particular, the church, Dietrich realized he had few answers. However, he intended to come up with some. Gerhard Jacobi, pastor of Berlin's Kaiser Wilhelm Memorial Church, had asked Dietrich to address a gathering of pastors at his home at the end of April. Dietrich was determined to have a Christian response to the Aryan Paragraph when he spoke to the pastors.

A week before the Aryan Paragraph was to go into effect, Hitler called for a boycott of Jewish stores and businesses across Germany. At a rally in Berlin that day, Joseph Goebbels, Nazi Minister of Enlightenment and Propaganda, railed against the Jews and all they had done to undermine Germany. He talked of "Jewish atrocity propaganda" and how the Jews controlled all foreign newspapers and were printing lies that hurt the image of their loving *führer*, Adolf Hitler. These must be stopped, he said. It was time for Germans to rise up against Jews and show them they must stop printing such falsehoods. Of course, most Jews had nothing to do with printing newspapers, but that didn't seem to matter to those listening to Goebbels's speech. They were angry and took to the streets with placards that read, "Germans, defend yourselves! Don't buy from Jews!" Goebbels's hate-filled tirade sickened Dietrich.

While German citizens took to the streets with placards, Nazi storm troopers (SA), the Nazis' paramilitary force, clad in their distinctive brown uniforms, fanned out onto city streets across Germany. Through intimidation and bullying they tried to stop customers from entering Jewish businesses. They also painted the Star of David on the windows of Jewish businesses, along with the word *Jude* (Jew).

Dietrich was proud of his ninety-year-old grandmother, Julie Bonhoeffer, who despised the Nazis and their handling of the situation. She decided to go shopping at her favorite store in Berlin, Kaufhaus des Westens, the world's largest department store. It also happened to be a Jewish-owned business. When she reached the store, Julie calmly walked up to the cordon of storm troopers positioned to stop people from entering. She shooed them aside, saying, "I have always shopped where I wanted to, and you will not change that!" Then she added indignantly, "All this nonsense about Jews and propaganda." With that she walked right into the store.

On April 11, as Dietrich worked to come up with a Christian response to the latest round of Nazi edicts, he received word that Gerhard Leibholz's father had died. Dietrich's twin sister, Sabine, wrote asking Dietrich to preach at her father-in-law's funeral. Dietrich was uncertain about this. Gerhard's father had been Jewish and, unlike his son, had not converted to Christianity. Dietrich found himself in a difficult situation. He wanted to honor his sister and brother-in-law's wishes, but now the Aryan Paragraph was in full effect. Given the emotional state Germany had been whipped into, a Christian pastor preaching at the funeral of an unconverted Jew could have repercussions for the Protestant church as it sought to clarify its response to the Nazis. Dietrich consulted his church superintendent, who advised him to stay away from the funeral. He followed the superintendent's advice.

The Nazis continued to persecute Jews. On April 22, they issued an edict banning Jews from serving as patent lawyers and Jewish doctors from accepting state-run insurance. Then, on April 25, the number of Jewish children who could go to school was severely reduced.

As Dietrich observed what was happening to the Jews, he was reminded of his time in the United States, where he had witnessed firsthand the plight of the blacks there. He thought back to his experience visiting Washington with Frank Fisher from Union Theological Seminary. The Jim Crow laws in the South had forbidden them, as a white man and a black man, from sitting together in a restaurant or riding on the same bus or tram car. The blacks couldn't even use the same restrooms. Dietrich had found the situation grotesque, especially in such a modern country as the United States. The phrase "separate but equal" was used to justify the segregated system, but Dietrich had seen enough in the United States to know that it was a sham. Black people in the United States were disadvantaged in every way compared to whites. And now in Germany, he saw the same system of segregation being put in place by the Nazis. This time, though, it was Jews who were the target of systematic segregation. Dietrich became more determined than ever to speak out about it.

Already many German pastors had given in to Nazi demands for the church, while other pastors and church members were confused about how to respond. On the one hand, Hitler talked about rebuilding a strong Christian country, bringing back morals, and eliminating God-hating communists. On the other hand, many of the Nazi ideals were harsh and went against the clear teachings of Jesus, particularly those found in His Sermon on the Mount. As far as the church and the Jewish question went, many pastors felt it a reasonable compromise that Jewish Christians should have their own pastors and worship in their own churches. What could the harm be? It wasn't as though Hitler was telling them that the Jews could not go to church, just that they should separate themselves from Aryan Christians.

When Dietrich had finished drafting a Christian response to the Aryan Paragraph, he titled his essay *The Church and the Jewish Question*. He intended to present it at the upcoming pastors' gathering.

Many important pastors were in attendance at the gathering at Gerhard Jacobi's residence. Twenty-seven-year-old Dietrich pulled a copy of the essay from the breast pocket of his jacket, unfurled the pages, and began to address the meeting. He spoke about the three ways in which the church should respond to any government. The first response was to speak out when a government tried to do things that went against the clear teachings of Jesus Christ. The second response was to help church members who had been victims of a corrupt government. As he laid out this point, several of the pastors present stood and walked out in protest. Undeterred, Dietrich moved on to the church's third response, which was to help anyone who was a victim of government repression, even if he or she was not part of the Christian community.

Dietrich paused for a moment to let the remaining pastors take in the full meaning of what he was saying: that the church should help Jewish people fight against any discrimination by the Nazi Party. Then Dietrich concluded, "What is at stake is by no means the question whether our German members of congregations can still tolerate church fellowship with the Jews. It is rather the task of Christian preaching to say: here is the church, where Jew and German stand together under the Word of God; here is the proof whether a church is still the church or not."

More pastors stood and walked out, but Dietrich stood his ground. Since visiting Rome and observing the Catholic church nine years before, he'd spent thousands of hours thinking and writing about the true meaning and nature of the church. For Dietrich, the church was made up of people from all ages, races, countries, and denominations. If any group called itself God's church but did not welcome all of these people inside, it was not really God's church, just a building filled with a group of self-important people.

After delivering his essay to the pastors, Dietrich began to regret that he had not followed his own advice more closely with regard to the church's third response. He realized he had allowed himself to be swayed by fear when he declined to preach at Gerhard's father's funeral. He promised himself that he would not let fear sway his actions again.

Dietrich also had *The Church and the Jewish Question* published. The publication coincided with still more Nazi restrictions on the Jews. Jewish dentists were barred from accepting state-run insurance, and Jews were purged from cultural organizations throughout Germany. But the Jews were not the only ones Nazis set their sights on. Trade unions in Germany were abolished, and the remaining political parties in the country were outlawed, making the Nazi Party the only political party allowed. Adolf Hitler was now Germany's dictator.

The next act in the Nazis' *Gleichschaltung* policy was the "Action against the Un-German Spirit." Universities across the country were to become centers of German nationalism. As such, they needed to be purged of Jewish intellectualism as well as any other "degenerate" ideologies that might undermine the pure German spirit and the affirmation of traditional German values.

This purge of universities began in spectacular fashion on the evening of May 10, 1933. On that night in most university towns across Germany, right-wing student groups gathered at the universities for torchlight parades and rallies. At the University of Berlin, where Dietrich still lectured in theology, nearly forty thousand people gathered at Hegelplatz at the rear of the university and marched across campus carrying flaming torches to the public square at Opernplatz, where a huge bonfire had been set ablaze. In the glow of the flames they listened as Goebbels delivered another fiery, emotional address. "No to decadence and moral corruption! Yes to decency and morality in family and state! I consign to the flames the writings of Heinrich Mann, Ernst Gläser, Erich Kästner." With that, he began to toss books onto the bonfire. The crowd, in a frenzy over Goebbels's speech, tossed more books onto the fire.

Books by Jewish authors like Albert Einstein were not the only ones burned. Books by other German authors whose work the Nazis considered degenerate were also burned, including works by Karl Marx, Bertolt Brecht, August Bebel, Thomas Mann, and Erich Maria Remarque. (Remarque was the author of *All Quiet on the Western Front*, the film version of which had touched Dietrich deeply when he saw it in the United States.) Books deemed to have a "corrupting foreign influence," including books by Ernest

Hemingway, Jack London, H. G. Wells, Theodore Dreiser, and Helen Keller, were also burned.

When he heard of the book burning at the University of Berlin, Dietrich was deeply troubled. He'd hoped for a better response from the university students, but in the face of so much Nazi propaganda, the students had given in to their base instincts.

During the summer of 1933, things began to change quickly in the German Protestant church. Those pastors who had aligned themselves and their congregations with the Nazis now called themselves "German Christians," and the faith they practiced was termed "Positive Christianity," a mix of Christian dogma and Nazi idealism. And now these German Christian pastors wanted to exercise more power over the church in Germany. Hitler helped them out by putting forward his personal adviser on church matters, an armed forces chaplain named Ludwig Müller, to be the Reich bishop. As such, he would be the head of the German Christian churches, coordinating their affairs and integrating them with the Nazis. The German Christian pastors quickly elected Müller as the new Reich bishop, despite the best efforts of Dietrich and a number of other important Protestant leaders who tried to persuade the pastors not to vote for Müller.

On Sunday, July 2, 1933, the German Christian congregations held services of thanksgiving at which a special message from Adolf Hitler was read from every pulpit. "All those who are concerned for the safe structure of our church in the great revolution of these times, must . . . feel deeply thankful that the state should have assumed, in addition to all its tremendous tasks, the great load and burden of reorganizing the church."

A shudder ran down Dietrich's spine as he read Hitler's words to the German Christians. The Nazis were now firmly in control of Germany's Protestant church. The question for Dietrich and other pastors now became how to respond to this situation. Was there still a place in Germany for the real, non-Nazi Christian church? What shape should this church take? And would the Nazis allow such a church to exist outside their direct control? Despite his best efforts, Dietrich had been unable to turn back the Nazi advance in taking control of the Protestant church. Now he wondered what the next challenge for him might be.

Chapter 11

England

In the fall of 1933, Dietrich was asked to take on the job of pastoring two churches in London, England. The two churches were under the same umbrella organization as the German church in Barcelona. At first Dietrich wasn't eager for the job. He knew he was needed in the fight against Nazi intrusion into the Christian church. Yet as he thought and prayed about the situation, Dietrich realized he could do a lot of useful things from outside of Germany. He could serve as a spokesperson to the world about what was going on, and he could help raise support for German Christians resisting the "synchronization" of the church with the Nazis.

On October 17, 1933, Dietrich found himself standing outside a large, old brick house in Forest

Hill, a southern suburb of London. He looked up at the second floor, where a visiting pastor told him he would be staying. "Just the two rooms," the man said, "although they're very large. The rest of the house is used as a German-speaking school, so you'll have the place to yourself at night."

Dietrich smiled and picked up his suitcase. "I'm sure it'll be fine," he responded. The house, though, lacked German precision. Even from the outside Dietrich could see that the window frames didn't line up, leaving gaping holes for the wind to whip through. Sure enough, the house was drafty and cold, and it had no central heating. The only heat came from two coin-operated gas heaters that emitted a weak flame. Dietrich joked that he had to sit on top of one of the heaters to feel any warmth.

Still, most of Dietrich's work was done away from the house. Dietrich was in charge of two very different German-speaking congregations. One church, located in Sydenham, included about forty people, most of whom worked at the German embassy in London. The other congregation, St. Paul's in London's East End, consisted of working-class German immigrants. Some of these people spoke only German, while their children tended to speak English. Dietrich was happy to pastor these two different groups. He loved both the intellectual stimulation of keeping up with the embassy staff and the challenge of helping the poorer, downtrodden immigrants at St. Paul's.

Life in London developed into an easy pattern for Dietrich. He had sermons to prepare and church members to visit. He also had weddings, funerals, and baptisms to officiate—all the usual pastoral duties Dietrich enjoyed so much. There was also another side to his work. Each morning Dietrich scoured *The Times* newspaper looking for information on Germany. It was hard to know what was true and what wasn't, as the Nazis were excellent at propaganda. Throughout the day he often talked with his mother on the telephone and with fellow pastors or his brothers. The news he gathered from these conversations was alarming. Just before Dietrich left Germany, a new law was passed stating that spouses of Jews were to be treated as if they were also Jewish. Dietrich was concerned even more about his sister Sabine, her husband Gerhard, and their two daughters.

Within days, another law was enacted so that Jews and their spouses could no longer attend entertainment or cultural events, such as art shows, movies, and book readings. Hitler insisted that this was done to protect Germans from their enemies both inside the country and around the world. He also played on German fears of the Soviet Union and how communism could spill over into Germany from there. To Dietrich's dismay, most Germans didn't notice that in an attempt to save themselves from communism, they had allowed a government just as harsh, if not harsher, to take root.

Also at the time Dietrich left Berlin for London, control of German newspapers had been handed over to the Nazi Party, and all Jewish journalists had been fired. "How could they be trusted to report the news

accurately?" Hitler asked. "After all, Jewish report-
ers do not tell the truth and are easily influenced by
communists."

Stranger news followed, though Dietrich had
no trouble believing it. The official German church
deemed the Bible "too Jewish" and decreed that all
references to Jews must be removed from it. Of course,
this meant that the entire Old Testament, the story of
the Jews, had to go, including the beautiful psalms
read in church each Sunday. Jesus was declared to
be "our greatest Aryan hero." The fact that he was
Jewish was completely ignored. Even hymns that
had Old Testament words in them like *Jehovah*, *halle-
lujah*, and *hosanna* had to go. That did not leave many
approved hymns.

Each morning *The Times* delivered more ominous
news. Those churches not aligned with the Nazis
were growing weaker by the day. Reich Bishop Ludwig Müller had already broken an earlier promise
and now agreed that all Protestant youth associa-
tions should be rolled into the Hitler Youth Movement. At the same time, Hitler said in a speech, "I
belong to no confession. I am neither Protestant nor
Catholic. I believe only in Germany." Dietrich found
it incredible that a man who did not even profess to
be a Christian was reshaping the church in his image.

For Dietrich, the last straw came when Ludwig
Müller announced that the church in Germany had
given up any struggle against the Aryan Paragraph,
which banned Jews from worshiping in Christian
churches. At the same time, the Reich bishop issued

the "Decree for the Restoration of Orderly Conditions in the German Evangelical Church." The title sounded innocent enough, but this made it illegal for anyone or any publication to discuss or mention anything about a struggle between the church and the führer. Now every time Dietrich made a phone call home to talk about what was happening in the church, he was committing a crime against the state.

To help put his time in England to best use, Dietrich flew to Germany every six weeks or so. His aim was to carry information back and forth so the outside world would know what was going on inside Germany and so that his Christian friends in Germany would be encouraged knowing that others were working hard to help them. Each time he returned to Germany, Dietrich heard of more pastors who had been jailed or had had bricks or bombs thrown through their windows by Nazi thugs.

Dietrich also hosted many Christian friends visiting England for various reasons. Among them was his friend and fellow pastor Franz Hildebrandt, who stayed for three months. Dietrich was delighted to have Franz around, and the two of them spent hours together praying and planning how to best help their fellow Christians and the German Jews.

One morning in late fall 1933, Dietrich's cause received a tremendous boost—just the break he'd been praying for. Dietrich was invited to meet that morning with Bishop George Bell, the Church of England's Bishop of Chichester. He had seen Bishop Bell from afar at interchurch conferences and always admired him. Now he wondered whether the bishop could help with the church situation in Germany. Dietrich and George Bell met at the bishop's church chambers in Chichester. Dietrich immediately liked the bishop, who had a keen interest in Christian affairs outside his own church and his own country. The two men soon learned to trust each other and became firm friends and allies.

Christmas was a busy time for Dietrich. He produced a Nativity play for the church and entertained many visitors in his two-room parsonage. By now his mother had sent over Dietrich's piano and several other large pieces of furniture and had hired a maid for him. This amused Dietrich, especially since the maid could not control the constant scampering of mice throughout the house. Nothing could. In the end, Dietrich and Franz gave up trying and placed all their food supplies in large tin cans. At night they watched as the mice scurried frantically. This became a conversation starter when visitors joined them for musical evenings.

All was not fun, however. Dietrich was playing a dangerous game, supplying Bishop Bell with specific information on what the Nazis were up to in Germany. He got much of this information from his brothers-in-law, Hans von Dohnanyi, a lawyer in the Reich Ministry of Justice, and Rüdiger Schleicher in the newly formed Reich Air Travel Ministry, as well as from extended-family contacts. Bishop Bell published the information Dietrich passed along in a stream of letters to the editor in *The Times*. It wasn't long before Dietrich's activities drew the attention of German church leaders in Berlin. Bishop Theodor Heckel was in charge of all German pastors serving in foreign countries. He visited England, arriving the day after Dietrich's twenty-eighth birthday, to meet with seven pastors from the various German churches in London.

Bishop Heckel's intentions were plain. He had come to get the pastors to sign an agreement declaring their allegiance to the German Reich church. The bishop started the meeting on a positive note, talking about all the wonderful things going on in Germany, how their beloved führer had taken the church youth groups under his wing, and how church leaders were really against the Aryan Paragraph and were just waiting for the right time to say so openly. He also talked about how the church, with the blessing of the Third Reich, had an unprecedented opportunity to win converts. But there was a darker side to his conversation. The bishop pointed out how unfortunate it would be if any of the London pastors were to commit treason by passing on to English church leaders, and in particular Bishop George Bell, information they believed to be true but clearly was not.

The meeting was held over to the next day, and Dietrich left the first session with a sense of doom. Throughout the meeting he had spoken truthfully, forcefully, and respectfully about his feelings with regard to the Reich church, so there was no doubt about where he stood.

The following morning, Bishop Heckel met with Bishop Bell. Dietrich knew that the German bishop planned to pressure the English bishop to stay out of the German church's business. Dietrich was confident there was no chance of that happening.

That afternoon the seven London pastors resumed their meeting with Bishop Heckel, who was in a dark mood. Dietrich knew that the meeting with Bishop Bell had not gone well. This time the bishop dispensed with pleasantries and insisted the pastors all sign the document of allegiance. If they refused to do so, Bishop Heckel threatened to have their German citizenship stripped from them. In the face of this threat, Dietrich and two other pastors stood and walked out. Dietrich was glad to learn that not one of the seven pastors in London signed the document.

A week later, Dietrich was summoned to Berlin for a private meeting with Bishop Heckel. At the meeting Dietrich stood his ground and again forcefully and respectfully put forward his beliefs about how he considered the Reich church to be engaging in heresy by combining Christianity with Nazi ideals. As far as he was concerned, the two could not coexist in the church.

It was clear to Dietrich that it was impossible for a true Christian pastor trying to live by the Bible to work with the Nazified German church. His view was becoming increasingly clear to other Christian leaders in Germany, including Karl Barth. In late May 1934, delegates from various Protestant churches around Germany met in Barmen to discuss their next step. This was a bold and decisive move. The delegates decided to form their own church structure and to be called the Confessing Church, after Jesus' words in Matthew 10:32: "Whosoever therefore shall confess me before men, him will I confess also before my Father which is in heaven" (KJV).

Dietrich was not at Barmen, but from London he was in constant phone contact with those who were. He knew the die had been cast. There was now no turning back. Dietrich and his fellow pastors had defied Hitler and shown the truth about the German church. When people suggested the Confessing Church had broken away from the German church, Dietrich corrected them. In his thinking, it was the German church that had steadily moved away from the clear teachings of Christ, and it was the Confessing Church that held true to His teaching.

Hitler did not immediately respond to this challenge from the church, and Dietrich soon learned he had other things on his mind. One month later on June 29, 1934, Operation Hummingbird, or as it quickly became known, the Night of the Long Knives, was carried out. On that night and on into next day many top Nazi officials and other enemies of Hitler and the Nazis were brutally murdered by the SS, the Nazi Secret Police.

Hitler tried desperately to keep the killings secret, but news of the deaths seeped out, first one, then another. Hitler eventually took responsibility for ordering the deaths of sixty-one people, including Ernst Röhm, the leader of the SA, the Nazi paramilitary wing. Dietrich was shocked by the news of the killings. He soon learned from his brother-in-law Hans that the Ministry of Justice believed that many more than sixty-one had been killed, perhaps as many as four hundred people.

The German public clamored for an explanation of the killings. On July 13, 1934, Hitler gave a speech to "clarify" why he had ordered so many executions without trials. The speech was broadcast nationally and was replayed on the BBC.

Dietrich sat by the radio, trying to fathom what was happening to his beloved country. He had been expecting something like this, and the brutality sickened him. He listened as Hitler declared,

> In this hour I was responsible for the fate of the German people, and thereby I became the supreme judge of the German people! . . . I gave the order to shoot the ringleaders in this treason, and I further gave the order to cauterize down to the raw flesh the ulcers of this poisoning of the wells in our domestic life. . . . Let the nation know that its existence—which depends on its internal order and security—cannot be threatened with impunity by anyone! And let it be known for all time to come that if anyone raises his hand to strike the state, then certain death is his lot.

As Dietrich gleaned more information from his sources in Germany, it appeared that Hitler had ordered the killing to appease German army generals and win their support. Hitler had learned that the generals were unhappy with the SA, and in particular its leader, Ernst Röhm, who was pushing for the army to be absorbed by the SA. By having Röhm and a number of other Nazi leaders murdered, Hitler crushed the power of the SA and secured the loyalty of the generals. But Hitler had not been content to just crush Röhm and the SA. He had used the opportunity to settle scores with many of his enemies by having them murdered too.

The Night of the Long Knives had another effect: it struck fear into the heart of every German.

Dietrich learned from his brother-in-law Hans that Hitler knew President Paul von Hindenburg was on the verge of death. He wanted to shore up his hold on power through gaining the support of the generals before the president died. On August 2, 1934, the eighty-six-year-old president of Germany died. Hindenburg had been an old and ineffectual leader in his last years, and Hitler was determined that there would be no new German president. He declared that the title of president would remain vacant out of respect for Hindenburg and that he, Adolf Hitler, would assume all of the responsibilities that had previously belonged to the president.

The nation was now firmly in the dictator's hands. No man or political office stood between Hitler and whatever he wanted to do. Hitler's first act was to require every member of the armed forces to swear a personal oath of loyalty to him. They would go wherever he pointed and do whatever he required of them.

On August 26, 1934, Dietrich found himself on the tiny island of Fanø, off the west coast of Denmark.

The setting was enchanting. Tiny wooden cottages with bright green sod roofs dotted the landscape, while wildflowers bloomed in the gardens. But Dietrich was not on Fanø to enjoy the scenery. He was attending a conference of the World Alliance of Churches where he was scheduled to give one of the keynote addresses and direct the International Youth Conference.

The conference was held against a background of tense change, not only in Germany but also in other parts of Europe. A month before, on July 25, 1934, a group of Austrian Nazis had stormed the Austrian chancellery building and shot Chancellor Engelbert Dollfuss. Over one million people attended his funeral in a show of support against the rise of the Nazis in Europe. Fearing that Hitler would move to annex Austria following the assassination, Italian dictator Benito Mussolini sent troops to the Austrian border as a warning to Germany to keep her hands off Austria, an Italian ally.

The Fanø conference was much as Dietrich had expected it to be. Some church leaders from around the world, including his friend Bishop George Bell and Swedish Bishop Valdemar Ammundsen, saw the growing threat of war in much the same light as Dietrich did. It was no surprise on the morning of August 28 when Dietrich addressed the conference on the subject of peace. His sermon was passionate and forthright. "There is no way to peace along the way of safety. . . . Peace is the opposite of security. . . . Peace means giving oneself completely to God's commandment, wanting no security, but in faith and obedience laying the destiny of the nations in the hand of Almighty God. Battles are won not with weapons but with God," Dietrich declared to the assembly.

While the conference delegates were stirred by Dietrich's preaching, most of them believed he was exaggerating the threat Hitler and the Nazis posed. As a result, Dietrich left Fanø frustrated that the World Alliance of Churches had not cut ties with the Reich church and would maintain "friendly" contact with its leaders. To Dietrich this was making a pact with the devil.

Back in London, Dietrich felt his time in England was almost over. He received word that the new Confessing Church in Germany intended to set up a seminary to train young pastors, and Dietrich was invited to be its director. This was the kind of challenge he was looking for. It would give him a way to influence many young men who would be at the forefront of the Confessing Church's battle with the Third Reich. It also meant that Dietrich would be leaving the safety of England to return to an increasingly dangerous situation, but issues of personal safety were far from his mind. Fellow Christians in Germany needed him, and Dietrich longed to be with them. On April 15, 1935, after a year and a half in England, Dietrich returned to Germany.

Chapter 12

Finkenwalde

Dietrich stood outside the old manor house. It was just what he needed—almost. The place was large enough and had plenty of grounds for growing crops and for sporting activities, but it was dilapidated. Railings hung off the stairs, windows were broken, birds nested in the fireplaces, and a large square addition gave the building a strange, unbalanced look. Still, he realized, it would have to do. The house had one big advantage—it was located in the tiny town of Finkenwalde in Pomerania, near the northeastern tip of Germany, far away from prying Nazi eyes. Dietrich was hopeful that the new Confessing Church seminary could exist there undetected, or at least ignored because of its isolation.

Once the decision was made to use the manor house at Finkenwalde, twenty-three students set to work transforming it into a seminary. A lot of scrubbing, sawing, hammering, and painting was needed before the place was fit to live in. Once it was habitable again, furniture was needed. Dietrich had his piano shipped in directly from London, and he went to Berlin to fetch his vast book collection to start the library. Once news of the seminary spread around the Pomeranian countryside, offers of help flooded in. The Pomeranians were traditional folk, not impressed with the Nazis. They happily contributed vegetables, sides of meat, and spare furniture to help anyone opposing the Nazis.

Dietrich had spent many years thinking about what should go into a well-rounded education for pastors. Having been a theology student himself, as well as a theology lecturer, he felt something was missing. Theology students came away with a lot of information in their heads and the ability to read Greek and Latin. But Dietrich had his doubts that they were really ready to lead a church congregation. Now that he was in charge of a seminary, he intended to try a new approach. He had six months to take the twenty-three theology graduates—twenty-two men and one woman—enrolled in the seminary and get them thinking and acting like pastors. His approach hadn't been tried in a Protestant church in Germany, and its strictness startled many of the students.

Each morning the students awoke, washed, and dressed in silence. Since they were bunked ten to a room and shared two bathrooms, this routine was an exercise in cooperation. Once washed and dressed, the students headed downstairs for a Bible reading, the singing of a hymn, and prayer. This was followed by a simple breakfast, and then it was time for each student to head back upstairs and meditate on a single Bible verse for a half hour. The students were told not to come back downstairs until they understood how the verse was relevant to the day ahead.

Many students complained to Dietrich that this routine was a waste of time. They thought that they should be getting on with the business of learning how to be pastors. Dietrich patiently explained that preaching and teaching were useless unless you were able to hear directly from the God you preached about. As the students got accustomed to the routine, the complaining gradually subsided. The rest of the day was spent learning practical things like how to conduct a baptism, a wedding, or a funeral; how to comfort a widow or an orphan; and how to preach a sermon or lead a Bible study.

There was plenty of fun along the way. The nights were long, and Dietrich often played the piano in the evenings. When the weather was warm enough, classes were held outside or even cancelled in favor of a hike in the beech woods or a swim in the nearby lake.

Slowly the seminary students gained confidence, both in their personal faith and in their ability to share it with others. This made Dietrich happy—happier than he'd ever been. He was also delighted to see deep friendships developing among the students, and quite unexpectedly became close friends with one of the students, Eberhard Bethge. Eberhard's father was a rural pastor, and Eberhard and Dietrich were from very different backgrounds, yet the two of them formed a firm friendship.

Dietrich also formed an unlikely friendship with a grandmother named Ruth von Kleist-Retzow. Ruth reminded him of his grandmother Bonhoeffer. She was feisty and opinionated, and she loved the Bible. She was also frustrated with the way so many pastors were kowtowing to the Nazis. Ruth was the daughter of a count and grew up in a palace at Oppern. She had married the wealthiest man in the district and had five children with him before being widowed at age twenty-nine. She was influential in the area and became a strong supporter of the seminary, bringing her grandchildren, Hans-Otto, Spes, Hans-Friedrich, Max, Ruth-Alice, and Maria, to seminary open meetings.

It would have been easy to shut off the outside world at Finkenwalde. Since few Nazi supporters lived in the area, there was no need to talk in whispers about what was happening in Germany. Yet Dietrich knew that Finkenwalde was only a resting place along the way. The Nazis would eventually catch up with them.

Even though he was far from Berlin in the countryside, Dietrich knew more about what was going on in the nation than most people. Each week he took the train back to Berlin, where he gave a theology lecture at the University of Berlin. While there, he learned about the state of affairs in the country from family and friends. His brother Klaus now served as a legal adviser at Deutsche Luft Hansa, Germany's national airline. He, along with his brothers-in-law Hans von Dohnanyi in the Reich Ministry of Justice and Rüdiger Schleicher at the Reich Air Travel Ministry, supplied Dietrich with all sorts of interesting tidbits about what Hitler and the Nazis were up to.

In October 1935, Dietrich's parents moved into a smaller home at 43 Marienburgerallee in the Berlin suburb of Charlottenburg. Once again, Dietrich was given a room on the top floor for his use when he was home. His grandmother Julie Bonhoeffer, now ninety-three years old, moved in with them.

Early in the new year, Julie died of pneumonia, and the entire family gathered to honor her. Dietrich preached at the funeral, and his words were clear and direct: "Her last years were clouded with great sorrow that she bore for the fate of the Jews among our people, a burden which she shared with them and a suffering which she, too, felt. She stemmed from another age, from another spiritual world, and this world does not descend with her into the grave. . . . This heritage for which we thank her lays duties upon us."

Dietrich keenly felt the loss of his grandmother. It was the end of an era, and he sensed it could be the last time the extended Bonhoeffer family was together in one place.

Back in Finkenwalde, Dietrich prepared the first group of students for graduation. On the night of his

thirtieth birthday, they all sat around the fire singing and telling stories. The students begged Dietrich
for stories of his time in Spain, the United States, and
London, and Dietrich happily obliged. After a while
the conversation shifted to how the students would
love to see more of the world themselves and meet
Christians from other countries and cultures. Suddenly the idea grew that they should all visit Sweden
together. Jokingly they suggested Dietrich give them
such a trip as a birthday gift from him to them. Dietrich loved the idea. It was just what he felt they all
needed to lift their spirits. A trip outside Germany
would help the students understand the church in a
wider context and let them see that the true church
around the world was standing with them.

Dietrich eagerly began planning. He didn't see
any sense in delaying the trip. He was concerned that
the Nazis would find out what they were up to and
forbid them to leave the country. As it was, travelers
were not allowed to take money out of the country,
and the seminary students would have to rely on the
kindness of Swedish Christians to board and feed
them.

Within a month of coming up with the idea, the
group was on its way to Sweden. The trip proved
to be a boost for everyone. Most of the students had
never traveled outside Germany, and it was eye-
opening for them to see that there were Christians
in another country who openly accepted them. As
they traveled, Dietrich posed the questions that had
influenced so much of his own thinking: What is the

church? Is it made up of people from the same country or cultural background, or is it made up of people who love God and follow the teachings of Christ? As he listened to the students' answers, Dietrich was satisfied that they were learning to see the true church and not the false version being presented to the world by the German Christian movement.

Regretfully, when the group returned to Germany, they discovered that their trip had been well documented. Dietrich had arranged the trip through his brother-in-law in the Justice Department. The group's plans had leaked out, and Bishop Heckel was not happy with Dietrich. The bishop carefully reviewed Dietrich's movements and decided he had violated a recent law banning university lecturers from leaving the country without a permit. As a result, Dietrich was dismissed from his weekly lecturing position at the University of Berlin. However, Bishop Heckel was reluctant to go any further in punishing Dietrich for his actions, at least for the moment. This was because an important event was about to take place that would put Germany on the world stage—the 1936 Olympic Games.

During the time leading up to the opening ceremony of the Olympic Games in Berlin on August 1, the Nazis did all they could to make Germany look like a peace-loving, just society. Dietrich watched as the "No Jews Allowed" signs were removed from the city's main tourist attractions. Other groups whom Hitler didn't think looked "German" enough, such as the Romani, Gypsies living on the outskirts of Berlin, were rounded up and placed in camps far away from the international visitors arriving for the games. German-Jewish athletes were barred from participating in the games, and many countries considered boycotting the event as a result. In the end, only the Soviet Union and Spain, where civil war had just broken out, were not present for the games.

The 1936 Berlin Olympics were spectacular. No expense was spared, and red and black swastika flags draped every building in the city. When the games were over, the *New York Times* declared that the Olympic Games put Germans "back in the fold of nations" and even made them "more human again."

But not for long. As soon as the Olympic Games were over, the Nazis reverted to persecuting non-Aryans and the Confessing Church. Even people who had been invaluable to the success of the games, like the head of the Olympic Village, Captain Wolfgang Fürstner, were not spared. Two days after the Olympics were over, Fürstner was dismissed from military service because of his Jewish ancestry. He killed himself that night.

Dietrich preached several times in Berlin during the bustle of the Olympics, but he was glad to get back to Finkenwalde. Following the graduation of the first seminary class, another group of about thirty young men took their place. But even in Finkenwalde, the post-Olympics crackdown could be felt. The Nazis made it illegal to read people's names out loud for prayer in church and for a church to send out any kind of newsletter or duplicated letter. All such communication had to be in the form of a personal letter, signed by hand. It was declared illegal for Confessing Church pastors to take up any kind of collection.

Such changes sapped the strength of many church workers. Dietrich did all he could to help them stand firm in the face of such opposition, but it was a discouraging task. Still, he did what he could, arranging for the wives of pastors arrested and taken to concentration camps to stay with his friend Ruth von Kleist-Retzow.

While running the seminary, Dietrich worked on the manuscript of a book of sermons based on Jesus' Sermon on the Mount. He planned to call the book *Discipleship*.

On July 1, 1937, Dietrich and his friend Eberhard were in Berlin visiting family and gathering information when they decided to visit Martin Niemöller, leader of the Confessing Church. Martin lived in the Berlin suburb of Dahlem. When Dietrich and Eberhard arrived at his house, they found only Dietrich's old friend Franz Hildebrandt and Martin Niemöller's wife, who recounted that the Gestapo (the Nazi secret police) had arrested Martin and taken him away only minutes before.

As the four of them sat at the dining table talking the situation over, several black Mercedes cars roared to a halt in front of the Niemöller house—the Gestapo were back. Dietrich, Eberhard, and Franz bolted out the back door of the house, right into the arms of a Gestapo officer who escorted them back inside and put them all under arrest.

Meanwhile, the Gestapo began searching the house. As they searched, an odd situation arose. Martin was a popular pastor, and as people came to the house to visit, they too were placed under arrest. Several hours passed, and Dietrich was surprised when he looked out the front window of the house and saw his parents' car drive by with his mother peering at the house from the rolled-down car window. The car drove past several times, and Dietrich wondered how his parents had found out what was going on.

Finally the Gestapo found a safe hidden behind a picture, from which they extracted a thousand marks. It was money Martin used to help pastors in emergencies. Pleased with their find, after seven hours, the Gestapo let all those under arrest go. Dietrich breathed a sigh of relief as he walked away from the house a free man.

Following Martin's arrest, Franz took over the preaching and pastoral duties at the church. He was just as fearless as Martin and met the same fate. On July 18, 1937, he was arrested by the Gestapo for reading aloud a prayer list containing the names of pastors sent to concentration camps and for taking up a collection in church. Dietrich was not present at the Dahlem church when Franz was arrested, but he heard about it later.

Franz was arrested at the end of the service. The congregation immediately began harassing the Gestapo officers arresting him. They screamed at the officers as they marched Franz outside and placed him in their car. They followed, surrounding the Gestapo car, beating on it. For some reason the car wouldn't start, and the Gestapo officers climbed out into the crowd and marched Franz off to jail on foot. The congregation followed, drawing everyone's attention to the actions of the normally secretive Gestapo. As a result, more people joined the protest procession. What Dietrich found amusing was that in the confusion, the Gestapo officers became disoriented and marched off in the opposite direction of Gestapo headquarters.

While Franz's arrest had its amusing side, Dietrich was concerned about his friend and rushed back to Berlin to see how he could help. In Berlin he learned that Franz had been sentenced to twenty-eight days in Plötzensee prison. Dietrich talked to his brother-in-law Hans about the situation, and Hans was able to pull some strings at the Ministry of Justice to get Franz released from prison two days early. This gave Franz a great advantage. His paperwork said he would be released from jail in twenty-eight days, but he was out in twenty-six. It was a common Gestapo practice to put a person in prison for a time and wait until he or she was released. Within minutes of release, the Gestapo would rearrest the person and ship him or her off to a concentration camp. Franz, whose mother was Jewish, would certainly have been subjected to torture and abuse in a concentration camp. But because of his early release, Franz slipped across the border into Switzerland before the Gestapo even knew he was free. Dietrich was relieved when he received a call informing him that Franz was safely in England, staying with Bishop Bell.

Soon after Franz's escape from Germany, the fifth group of seminary students graduated from their six-month course at Finkenwalde. Following graduation, Dietrich traveled to Göttingen to visit Sabine and her husband, Gerhard Leibholz. While in Göttingen, he received a phone call from Finkenwalde. It was bad news. The Gestapo had arrived and sealed the seminary doors. It was the end of an era. Dietrich knew there was no point in returning. Now he had to decide what was next.

Chapter 13

Crossroads

Heil Hitler! Long live the führer!" Dietrich and his friend Eberhard stood at the loft window of the Bonhoeffer home in Berlin and listened. Thousands of people were gathered along the parade route to celebrate Adolf Hitler's forty-ninth birthday, April 20, 1938. The din of the crowd echoed across the city while row upon row of soldiers stood at attention.

By now it appeared to Dietrich that Germany was gearing up for another war. Of course, many Germans didn't believe that Hitler had war on his mind, not even after the *anschluss*, or joining. A month before, Austria had ceased to exist as an independent nation and was now part of Germany. Through a mix of cunning, deceit, propaganda, and intimidation, Hitler had pulled off the takeover under the guise of uniting all German-speaking lands and territories with Germany. What amazed and disturbed Dietrich about the anschluss was how easily the Nazis had done it and how little other European nations had protested.

According to Dietrich's brother-in-law Hans, this was just the start. Secret sources had informed Hans that Hitler and the Nazis were recklessly determined to start a glorious war that would lead to Nazi domination of the world. It would be a very different war from the previous one. This time Hitler would be in charge of everything, and there would be no consulting anyone under him. What the führer decided was all that mattered. A chill ran through Dietrich as he thought about it. What would happen to the Jews, the Romani, and all the other groups for which Hitler had a personal disdain? Would there be anywhere for them to hide?

Later that day, Dietrich listened to the führer's birthday address on the radio. He also learned of a "gift" Hitler had not mentioned on air. As a special present to himself, Adolf Hitler now required all Protestant pastors to swear a personal oath to him. Dietrich saw this as an opportunity to stand up for Jesus Christ. Most of the pastors saw it as a necessary act to continue their work.

Dietrich did not have to take the oath himself, as he was not a registered pastor, but he strongly urged the 150 graduates from the Finkenwalde seminary not to take it. Most of them, however, could see no real harm in taking the oath. This left Dietrich feeling disappointed and alone. Was he the only one who saw how evil Hitler and the Nazis were? Perhaps *he* was the one who was misguided. Dietrich didn't think so, but it was hard to keep encouraging young pastors who did not share his sense of urgency or doom.

Dietrich and Eberhard stayed at the Bonhoeffer home in Berlin, and from there traveled the country, trying to help pastors and their families cope with the challenges they faced. Many of them still believed that Hitler was good for Germany and that in time the church's problems would all be sorted out.

This view proved shortsighted. By September, tanks were parading through Berlin. Again, under the guise of uniting all German-speaking lands and territories with Germany, Hitler was demanding that large parts of Czechoslovakia populated by German-speaking people be handed over to Germany. However, the Czech government refused to comply, and rumor suggested that Germany would soon invade the country.

On September 9, 1938, Dietrich, accompanied by Eberhard, escorted his sister Sabine, her husband Gerhard, and their two daughters to the Swiss border. Hans had told them it was time to flee Germany. He had learned that Jews would soon be forbidden to leave the country. The Leibholz family crossed the border just in time. Once in Switzerland, they made their way to England, where Dietrich had arranged for Bishop George Bell and several other friends to help them get settled. Dietrich breathed a sigh of relief when he learned they were safely in England. He was even more delighted when he learned that Gerhard, a brilliant legal scholar, had been invited to lecture on political science at Magdalen College, Oxford. Gerhard also served as an adviser to Bishop Bell, who had recently become a member of the House of Lords in the British Parliament.

The imminent invasion of Czechoslovakia did not occur. The governments of France, Great Britain, and Italy intervened, and at a conference in Munich on September 30, a deal was struck. Czechoslovakia would cede to Germany the territory in which the Sudeten Germans lived. In return, Hitler declared that with the addition of Sudetenland to Germany, his goal of uniting all German-speaking lands and territories with Germany was complete. There would be no more territorial demands.

On the night of November 9, 1938, Nazi storm troopers and civilians went on a rampage throughout Germany, ransacking Jewish homes and shops and setting synagogues on fire. The rampage was quickly dubbed *Kristallnacht*, or the "Night of Broken Glass." At the time, Dietrich was in the mountains visiting a group of young pastors training in secret, and he did not learn about the rampage right away. When he did, he was not surprised. He'd seen it coming and was sad that the Confessing Church had not made more of a stand against Nazi hatred and violence. Some pastors did preach against the violence, and when they did, they were hauled off to prison. Generally though, most Confessing Church pastors no longer had the strength or the will to oppose Hitler and the Nazis.

The situation became a turning point for Dietrich. Until now he had put all his energy into helping the church confront the evils of the Nazis. Now he gave up hope that this would be enough. It was time to change tactics, and the change of tactics he began contemplating was joining his brother-in-law Hans in a secret conspiracy to overthrow Hitler's government. It was a bold move, but Hitler had to be stopped. He was a madman capable of spewing hatred and havoc far beyond the borders of Germany.

Hans no longer worked for the Ministry of Justice. He was now a supreme court judge in Leipzig. However, he traveled to Berlin once a week to lecture at the University of Berlin, as Dietrich had done until dismissed from the position. These weekly visits provided Hans the opportunity to meet with key friends and past colleagues who were happy to pass on to him information about what was going on deep inside Hitler's government. Hans told Dietrich that a number of high-ranking military members had already planned to carry out two coup attempts, but both had been thwarted by the fast-moving events of the time.

Dietrich felt he was at the biggest crossroads of his life. Should he move away from his role as an encourager of the Confessing Church and position himself to do whatever he could to help his brother-in-law in the plot to bring down the Nazis? Dietrich wrestled with his conscience. He talked to his parents and friends about the choice, but there was one man who understood him better than anyone else—Bishop George Bell. In early 1939, Dietrich obtained the necessary passes to travel to England.

In England, Dietrich was kept busy. He spent time with Sabine and Gerhard, as well as with his old friend Franz Hildebrandt. He also preached in his old parish churches in London and met with a number of German pastors Bishop Bell had helped escape to England. Dietrich traveled to Sussex to meet with Reinhold Niebuhr, who was visiting from the United States. Niebuhr had been a professor at Union Theological Seminary in 1930 when Dietrich had been there, and he was considered the United States' best theologian. Dietrich had a great time catching up with him, reminiscing about his time in New York, and talking about the challenges the church faced in Germany. And, of course, Dietrich spent time talking things over with Bishop Bell.

Yet for all his time and effort in England seeking clarity, Dietrich was still uncertain. It was clear that in the near future all German men of fighting age would be called up to join Hitler's military, and at thirty-three Dietrich was of fighting age. Yet from his experience watching *All Quiet on the Western Front* in New York with Jean Lasserre, Dietrich knew that he could not take up arms against his fellow man. He knew he would have to refuse military service. He also knew it would mean more turmoil for the Confessing Church if one of its leaders became a conscientious objector. This was one of the issues he talked over with Bishop Bell. The bishop offered helpful advice, but Dietrich was unable to come to a long-term decision.

The short term was different, however. During his visit with Niebuhr, Dietrich was invited to give a series of lectures in New York. It seemed a perfect opportunity for him. It would get him away from Germany and give him time to think things through. It would also give him the opportunity to speak to the world about what was happening in Germany.

Indeed, just as Dietrich decided to accept the invitation to go to the United States, news reached England that Hitler had broken the agreement he had made with Great Britain, France, and Italy just six months before. On March 16, 1939, German troops marched into Prague, Czechoslovakia, and took over the country.

Back in Germany, Dietrich made preparations for his lecture series in New York. His brother Karl-Friedrich, who had been asked to give a series of physics lectures in Chicago, decided to travel with him. On June 2, the two Bonhoeffer brothers boarded an airplane at Tempelhof Airport in Berlin and flew to London. There they took a train to Southampton and boarded the SS *Bremen* for the trip to New York.

The voyage across the Atlantic was a restless one for Dietrich. He knew he was headed to safety and security and away from the threat of war and doom, but he was not happy. He could not shake the idea that he was running away, leaving his brothers and sisters in the Confessing Church to fend for themselves. No matter how he tried to look at the situation, Dietrich could find no peace. By the time the *Bremen* slipped into New York Harbor, he wondered whether he'd made a mistake.

The next morning Dietrich had breakfast with Dr. Henry Smith Leiper, who was organizing Dietrich's visit. It was a painful meeting. Dr. Leiper was eager to plan a lecture tour while Dietrich was wondering whether he should be there at all.

A week later Dietrich had a second meeting with Dr. Leiper, at which he was to present the outlines of the lectures he planned to give. The night before, he had wandered the streets of New York City alone. He longed to hear what was going on at home in Germany. Had the Confessing Church found someone to replace him as coordinator of training? How was his friend Eberhard getting on? And his parents? And what about the conspiracy to be rid of Hitler that his brother-in-law was involved in?

Dietrich realized that if he stayed in the United States he would have to get used to unanswered questions. It was difficult enough getting information out of Germany now, since those who wrote letters to people outside the country risked their lives. How much worse would it be when war broke out and there was no communication? Could he stand on the sidelines lecturing about theology while his brothers and sisters in the church in Germany suffered? Dietrich didn't think he could do that.

In the end, Dietrich realized he would have to tell Dr. Leiper that he wanted to go back home to

Germany to face war and hardship shoulder to shoulder with his church and family. He wrote in his journal, "At the end of the day I can only ask God to give a merciful judgement on today and all its decisions. It is now in his hand."

Many of Dietrich's friends and colleagues in the United States tried to convince him to stay. War seemed inevitable, they argued, and in the United States he would be safe and could lend a helping hand to rebuild the German church when the war was over. Dietrich agreed that their arguments were all reasonable, but he'd made up his mind. On July 7, 1939, just over a month from the time they'd left Berlin, Dietrich and Karl-Friedrich, who had finished delivering his physics lectures in Chicago, boarded a ship in New York. They were on their way home to an uncertain future.

Chapter 14

Conspiracy

Nearly three months had passed since Dietrich left the United States, and he and Karl-Friedrich were out for a bicycle ride near their parents' home. Suddenly sirens sounded all over Berlin. "This can mean only one thing," Karl-Friedrich said grimly.

Dietrich nodded. "War! God help us all."

The two brothers peddled back to the Bonhoeffer house on Marienburgerallee and joined their mother in the living room. She was listening to the radio. The voice of Adolf Hitler permeated the room. "We refuse all efforts to force us to recall the troops which have been sent for the protection of the Reich. . . . From now on, bombs will meet with bombs."

Soon Hans joined them. He now worked for Abwehr, German Military Intelligence, as he assisted

149

those involved in the conspiracy against Hitler and the Nazis. He had the latest information. That morning at 5:45, German troops began an invasion of Poland. The invasion was supposedly in response to a Polish attack on a German border post, but Hans had learned that this was a lie. Hitler had staged the attack. The only person killed was a German citizen whom the Nazis had killed to make it look like Polish soldiers had shot him.

Dietrich listened carefully as his brother-in-law spoke. Bombers from the *Luftwaffe*, the German air force, had launched wave after wave of bombing attacks against Warsaw, the Polish capital. They were also targeting road and rail junctions and Polish troops. Towns and villages were being bombed to create a mass of fleeing, terror-stricken civilians who would block the roads and hinder the flow of Polish reinforcements to the fighting. Meanwhile, two German army groups had invaded the country, one from Prussia in the north and the other from the new country of Slovakia in the south. These troops were accompanied by hundreds of *panzers* (German tanks) and were steadily capturing Polish territory.

Dietrich sighed deeply as he thought of all the Polish people being killed that day. Hitler's thirst for territory seemed unquenchable.

According to Hans, Poland had already requested immediate military assistance from France and Britain, with whom the country had a military alliance. But Hitler didn't think the British would intervene. He thought British Prime Minister Neville Chamberlain would push for a diplomatic solution and not resort to war. As far as Hitler was concerned, Great Britain was too weak to go to war with Germany.

"We will all pay for that arrogance," Dietrich said, sounding dejected. Those around him nodded.

Sure enough, Hitler had misjudged the British. Instead of pushing for a diplomatic solution, on Sunday, September 3, 1939, two days after the invasion of Poland, Britain and France declared war on Germany.

Dietrich sat quietly when he heard the news. It was like 1914 all over again. Once more Germany was at war with Britain and France. He was glad that many of his friends and his sister Sabine and her family had escaped in time. There was no telling when he would see them all again.

Dietrich studied his mother's face as she sat across the room from him. Paula looked worn. Dietrich was sure she was thinking of his brother Walter and wondering who else in the family might lose his or her life this time around.

The next day Dietrich received word that one of the 150 men who had graduated from the Finkenwalde seminary had been killed in the fighting in Poland. He feared that this was the first of many such deaths.

The declaration of war on Germany meant that Dietrich now had to find a way to move forward. He refused to fight in Hitler's army, but he did consider becoming a chaplain. He spoke with his mother's cousin, General Paul von Hase, commander of Berlin, and asked for his help. Paul did all he could, but the regulations were clear. A person must enlist in the army before being considered for chaplain duties. Dietrich knew he could never enlist in the army, but refusing the draft and enlistment carried the penalty of death—by beheading. Somehow Dietrich was not immediately called up for military service. This left him free to continue encouraging the Confessing Church pastors still left at their posts.

The declaration of war by Great Britain and France did not stop Hitler from invading Poland. Dietrich began to dread his brother-in-law's visits to the house. Every new piece of information Hans brought with him was more shocking than the last. Hans told how Hitler planned to turn the Poles into slaves and Poland into a huge labor camp. As far as Hitler was concerned, the Poles were subhuman and only good for work. Toward this end, the SS brutality in Poland was unfathomable. Under Hitler's orders, the SS had begun systematically killing Jews, clergymen, intellectuals, the nobility, and anyone who showed leadership potential. According to Hans, the Polish people were being so brutally dealt with by the SS that German officers and regular soldiers were sickened by what they saw.

Hans also related that it wasn't just the Poles who were on the receiving end of Nazi brutality. Hitler had also turned his focus on the extermination of "defective" Germans. According to Hans, children born with genetic defects and patients in hospitals deemed to be "unfit" were being secretly rounded up and executed by the Nazis.

Dietrich was stunned. The Nazis' brutal and murderous ways were beyond comprehension. How could Germans do such things to other human beings? Didn't they know they were tearing the fabric of German civilization to shreds with such barbarism? Hitler had to be stopped before Germany was completely destroyed.

Hans told Dietrich that he wasn't alone in that feeling. Many top German generals were so repulsed by what was happening they were planning to kill Hitler and his henchmen and stage a coup. Hans said he was willing to be part of any plot to do away with such evil. He also confided that he was keeping a record of all the atrocities Hitler and the Nazis had carried out so there would be no doubt as to their crimes when the war was over. His superior at Abwehr, Admiral Wilhelm Canaris, supported what he was doing. Hans reported that he'd already collected a lot of evidence, which he called his "Chronicle of Shame." The record included papers and other documents and film footage of many terrible things the Nazis had done in Poland.

By the end of September, Poland had surrendered, and Dietrich hoped that Hitler and the Nazis would stop their madness, at least for a while. But it was not to be. Dietrich learned from his brother-in-law that Hitler planned to follow up his success in Poland with surprise attacks on both Belgium and Holland, followed by attacks on France and then on England, Denmark, and Norway. It seemed almost too preposterous to be true, but Dietrich had learned enough by now not to underestimate Hitler's resolve or his bloodlust.

The main problem the conspirators faced revolved around the question of what would happen to Germany once Hitler was killed. Would the British and French, or the Russians, flood into Germany in retaliation for what the Nazis had done to Poland? Would they understand that not all Germans were aware of what was going on and did not support the Third Reich? These were difficult issues, and Germans who had connections with the outside world were needed to reach out to foreign countries and get their assurances that they would support the building of a democratic and peaceful Germany upon Hitler's assassination. In this regard, Hans had a serious proposal to put before Dietrich. If he could find a way to get Dietrich the necessary travel documents, would Dietrich be prepared to go and talk with Bishop Bell in England and his friends in Norway and Denmark in a bid to get their governments to work with the conspirators?

Dietrich considered the offer. Hans, his brother Klaus, and his brother-in-law Rüdiger Schleicher were all now active participants in the conspiracy. Dietrich had no problem encouraging them in their resistance, but joining them was a different matter. He told Hans that he would pray about it.

Meanwhile, in April 1940, German forces overran Denmark and Norway. While they were doing this, Hitler would announce the invasion date of Belgium and Holland to his officers, then change the date, and change it again. In fact, he changed the date nearly thirty times, throwing the assassination attempt, which was scheduled to take place right before the invasion was to start, into chaos. Finally on May 10, 1940, Hitler ordered the invasion of Holland and Belgium. As German troops rolled into both countries, there was no assassination. The German conspirators had lost their best opportunity.

German troops subdued Holland in just five days and then marched on through Belgium into France. A month later, on June 14, German troops marched into Paris. Three days later French Prime Minister Marshal Philippe Pétain asked for an armistice with Germany. Hitler had the same railway car in which the Germans had signed the 1918 Armistice removed from a museum in Paris and placed at the precise spot in the forest of Compiègne where it had been located in 1918. Hitler then sat in the same chair in the car that French Marshal Ferdinand Foch had sat in when he faced the defeated German representatives. Thus seated, Hitler faced the French representatives as France surrendered to Germany.

Dietrich and Eberhard were in the eastern Prussian town of Memel at the time, visiting one of the pastors trained at the Finkenwalde seminary. They were enjoying a cup of coffee at an outdoor café when they heard the announcement of France's surrender over the café's radio. People all around went wild with joy. Patrons climbed on their chairs and sang patriotic German songs. Someone raised his hand in salute of Adolf Hitler, and the others followed. "Heil

Hitler" echoed down the street. Dietrich stood and raised his hand too. Eberhard looked at him in shock. "What are you doing? Have you gone mad?"

Dietrich muttered, "I'm not crazy. Raise your arm like everyone else. There will be times when we have to make a stand, but not for this silly salute."

Eberhard hesitated and then raised his hand.

As Dietrich sang "Deutschland über Alles" ("Germany above All," the German national anthem), he realized that he had crossed the line. The decision had been made. Hitler and the Nazis would stop at nothing to gain more power and more territory, and Dietrich would do whatever he could to stop them, even if it meant pulling the trigger on the führer himself. He had thought about it from every angle, and his conscience was clear. Hitler and the evil he was perpetrating upon Europe had to be stopped by any means available. Dietrich was now part of the conspiracy.

In early August, Dietrich and Eberhard met with Hans and other members of the resistance within Abwehr. Admiral Canaris and the chief of staff, Colonel Hans Oster, were intent on overthrowing Hitler and the Nazis. Hans explained that Admiral Canaris wanted Dietrich to work out of Abwehr's office in Munich, where he would be out of the spotlight of Berlin. From there Dietrich would be sent on missions outside Germany to shore up support for the coup and inform the "enemy" of what was going on.

Dietrich also learned that Colonel Oster had warned the Dutch military before Hitler invaded, but they had taken no action because their government could not believe it possible that Germany would attack a peaceful nation. This gave Dietrich an inkling of the problems he would face in dealing with foreign powers. It was difficult for anyone outside Germany to fully understand the evil intentions of the führer.

Before the meeting was over, Dietrich had agreed to become a double agent for the resistance, working for German Military Intelligence while passing along information on the Allies. While awaiting his first assignment, Dietrich stayed with Ruth von Kleist-Retzow in the peaceful Pomeranian countryside. Dietrich worked on the new book he was writing, *Ethics.*

In October 1940, Dietrich learned that all the preparations were in place, and he moved to Munich, where he stayed with his aunt, Countess Kalckreuth. It wasn't an ideal situation, as her neighbors and acquaintances were curious about Dietrich and began asking questions about what he did. Soon a much better opportunity presented itself. Dietrich was invited to stay with the Benedictine monks of Ettal, about fifty miles south of Munich in the Bavarian Alps. The abbot, Father Johannes, was a member of the resistance and understood how valuable Dietrich was.

Living in the abbey at Ettal, Dietrich found himself very much at home. Although it was a Catholic order, many similarities existed between the abbey and the Finkenwalde seminary. Dietrich loved the morning prayers and the readings at mealtimes, along with times of silent meditation. He also loved the abbey's large, well-stocked library, where he studied, wrote, and awaited his first assignment for the resistance through the Munich office of Abwehr.

On February 24, 1941, Dietrich was sent on his first foreign assignment. He was to travel to Geneva, Switzerland, where he was to make contact with Protestant leaders outside Germany and inform them of the conspiracy to do away with Hitler. He would also try to find out what sort of peace terms the government that took over in Germany could come to with the Allies.

In Geneva, Dietrich met with Willem Visser 't Hooft, a Dutchman. As secretary general of the World Council of Churches, he had the ear of many influential leaders. Dietrich told him all about what was happening inside Germany, including the way the Nazis were exterminating "defective" Germans. He also explained to Visser 't Hooft how the conspiracy to get rid of Hitler had lost some of its momentum after Hitler's stunning victories in the west, especially the surrender of France. For many Germans this was a moment of pride as the humiliation they had endured twenty-two years before at the end of World War I was swept aside. Given Hitler's popularity in Germany following the event, many top military men involved in the coup attempt had lost their resolve. But Dietrich assured Visser 't Hooft that the conspiracy was gaining in strength again as more generals secretly got in touch with the resistance group inside Abwehr. Visser 't Hooft assured Dietrich that he would pass the information on and put out feelers as to the sort of peace terms the Allies might be willing to extend to a new government in Germany.

In Switzerland, Dietrich was free to write letters to his friends in other countries. He wrote to Sabine and Gerhard in Oxford, England, saying he missed them deeply and bringing them up to date on what was happening in Germany and with the family in Berlin. He also wrote to Bishop George Bell in London. In Geneva he visited Erwin Sutz, his Swiss friend from Union Theological Seminary in New York. And before leaving Switzerland, Dietrich traveled to Basel to visit Karl Barth. After a month away, Dietrich returned to Germany and reported on his Geneva meetings to Hans and Admiral Canaris.

Dietrich spent Easter 1941 with his parents at the summerhouse in Friedrichsbrunn. Just as he had during World War I, Dietrich found the surroundings relaxing and rejuvenating. War and Nazi mayhem all seemed so far away. While at Friedrichsbrunn, he found time to keep writing.

Dietrich was aware that Hitler was not content with the territorial gains he'd made in the west. Hitler had a deep disdain for the "eastern" races, which included the Poles and Slavs, and he was gearing up for a massive military attack in the east against the Soviet Union. This was known as Operation Barbarossa. By early June nearly three million German troops had amassed along Poland's border with the Soviet Union. In preparation for the attack, on June 6,

1941, Hitler issued an order to his military commanders known as the "Commissar Order." According to this order, the army was to shoot and kill on the spot all captured Soviet military leaders. No mercy was to be shown.

The Commissar Order sent shock waves through the German military ranks. In the invasion of Poland it had been the SS that carried out the ghoulish brutality against the Poles. Now Hitler expected regular soldiers to do that work for him. Such unprecedented brutality went against the ancient military code and sense of honor that military officers lived by. As a result, many more generals began seeking out the conspirators and offering their support for the assassination of Hitler and overthrow of the Nazis.

At the same time, word reached the resistance group within Abwehr that British Prime Minister Winston Churchill was reluctant to separate the Nazis from regular Germans. As far as he was concerned, all Germans should be treated as Nazis. This was not the news the conspiracy had hoped to hear. They wanted Britain and France to understand that there were those Germans who abhorred Hitler and were willing to risk their lives to bring him down but didn't want Germany to be destroyed and humiliated by the Allies, as had happened after World War I. They wanted peace and the opportunity to build a new, peaceful and democratic Germany.

As a result of the uncertainty about how the Allies would treat Germany if Hitler were killed, no assassination or coup attempt occurred before Hitler ordered German troops to attack the Soviet Union on June 22, 1941. Despite their reservations and deep disdain for Hitler and his orders, the dispirited generals led their troops into battle. Dietrich was discouraged that another opportunity had been lost.

By September 1941, something that Hans had long warned Dietrich about became a reality. Hitler was no longer content to kill only "defective" Germans. He had set his sights on systematically killing another group of German citizens—Jews and their relatives. According to Hans, Reinhard Heydrich, a high-ranking Nazi official, was putting together a plan to achieve this goal, which would start with Jews being forced to identify themselves by wearing a Star of David on their clothing. Dietrich was deeply distressed when he learned this. The utter evilness of Hitler and the Nazis overwhelmed him. They had turned the country he loved into hell.

Chapter 15

Work of a Spy

On September 2, 1941, Dietrich was riding in an overcrowded train back to Berlin after his second visit to Geneva. As he boarded the train, he noticed hollow-eyed men and women wearing yellow stars sewn onto their clothing. Dietrich took a deep breath and thought about the things Hans had warned him about regarding the Jews. In the week Dietrich had been away in Switzerland, a decree had been issued ordering all Jews over the age of six to identify themselves by wearing the Star of David with the word "Jude" on their outer clothing.

After explaining the details of his Geneva trip to Hans and Admiral Canaris, Dietrich reported back to the Abwehr office in Munich. He and another resistance worker named Justus Perels, a legal adviser to the Confessing Church, were assigned to collect all the information they could about the Jewish situation. They reviewed many highly confidential documents and made visits to the Rhineland, where Jews were already being rounded up and shipped east by train to concentration camps in western Poland. Dietrich and Justus's findings were contained in a thorough report they wrote detailing precise information about how the Gestapo and the SS were carrying out their operation of rounding up Jews and shipping them east.

Copies of the report were carried to Geneva, where they found their way to Allied governments and were shared with sympathetic military leaders inside Germany. Surely now, Dietrich thought, was the time to kill Hitler. As reports came back from the Soviet Union, where German troops were marching at a speedy clip toward Moscow, the pressure mounted to do away with Hitler.

On a personal level, Dietrich and many others did what they could to save Jews from falling into the hands of the Nazis. Across Germany many pastors, at great risk to themselves and their families, sheltered Jews in their homes. Dietrich became involved in what became known as Operation 7, a plan to save a group of seven Jews by helping them get across the border into Switzerland. The seven were friends of Admiral Canaris and Hans, and the plan called for them to be allowed across the border so they could tell the Swiss government how "well" the Nazis were treating Jews. There were those in the leadership of the Gestapo and SS who believed Jews should be expected to lie on behalf of the Nazis, so freedom for a small group of Jews going to Switzerland to speak well of the Nazis was an acceptable price for such an action. Of course, Hans and Admiral Canaris did not expect the group to speak well of the Nazis once in Switzerland. Quite the opposite. They wanted them to tell the Swiss the real truth of what was happening to Jews inside Germany.

The plan, however, proved more complex than Hans had expected. Not only had the escaping group of Jews grown to fourteen, but also Switzerland, a neutral country, was reluctant to accept a group of German Jews. Finally Dietrich and several other men, including Justus Perels, were asked to contact various church leaders in Switzerland and ask them to pressure their government in allowing the group to enter the country.

When this approach wasn't successful, Dietrich contacted his old friend Karl Barth for help. Eventually Barth was able to persuade the Swiss to take the group, but their decision came at a price. The Swiss government wanted a payment of a large amount of foreign currency to cover the costs of the Jews being in Switzerland, since they would not be able to work to support themselves. Hans went to work on securing the foreign currency. This was the riskiest part of the plan, as it was difficult to secretly secure and transfer foreign currency without the Gestapo noticing. Eventually Hans succeeded, and the fourteen Jews escaped to freedom in Switzerland. Dietrich was greatly relieved. He just wished that every other Jew in Germany and Nazi-controlled territory could attain such freedom.

Following Operation 7, Dietrich was forced to take a break from his work in November 1941 when he became ill with pneumonia. He moved to Ruth von Kleist-Retzow's estate in Pomerania to recuperate. As soon as he felt a little better, he resumed writing *Ethics*. It was difficult being away from the daily news Dietrich had received in Munich and Berlin. So much was happening with the conspiracy and the Nazi advance into the Soviet Union. Dietrich prayed the war would end soon, and for a while it looked like it might.

Throughout October 1941, many German generals involved in the conspiracy believed it was time to overthrow Hitler. They continued to be deeply troubled by the brutality of the SS. Even General Walther von Brauchitsch, the commander in chief of the German army, believed it was time for Hitler to be done away with. As a result, planning for a new coup to overthrow Hitler began. But things changed quickly during November. The German military suffered its first loss when the Russians routed German troops at Rostov as they advanced toward Stalingrad. Hitler was furious and ordered the German forces forward, no matter what the cost to the troops.

By December 2, the first German battalion reached the outskirts of Moscow. Then the vicious Russian winter descended, stalling the German advance in its tracks. The temperature plummeted to more than thirty degrees below zero. German soldiers, ill equipped for such extreme weather, began to die of frostbite, and the fuel in German tanks froze and rifles seized up. Then on December 6, Russian troops attacked the Germans with overwhelming force, causing the Germans to retreat as fast as they could through the frozen terrain.

Hitler was incensed that his armies were in retreat. He fired many of his top generals, including General Brauchitsch. Instead of appointing another commander in chief of the army, Hitler took over the role himself. The firing of General Brauchitsch and so many other German generals involved in the conspiracy brought the impending coup to a halt.

At the same time, on December 7, 1941, the Japanese bombed Pearl Harbor in Hawaii, bringing the United States into the war. Four days later, on December 11, Germany declared war on the United States.

With the United States now in the war and German troops mired in Russia, Dietrich was more convinced than ever that it was only a matter of time before Germany lost the war and Hitler was dealt with. As he thought about that day, he imagined what he would tell German Christians when the fighting was over. He came to the conclusion that every Christian, and the church as a whole, would have to examine their own hearts to see what part they had played in letting such evil loose on the world. It would not be good enough to point the finger at others who had done worse things. He put it this way in writing: "Confession of guilt happens without a sidelong glance at the others who are also guilty. This confession is strictly exclusive in that it takes all guilt upon itself."

With this in mind, Dietrich wrote a document he hoped that Christians in Germany would embrace after the war.

> The church confesses that it has witnessed the arbitrary use of brutal force, the suffering in body and soul of countless innocent people, that it has witnessed oppression, hatred and murder without raising its voice for the victims and without finding ways of rushing to their help. It has become guilty of the lives of the Weakest and most Defenceless Brothers and Sisters of Jesus Christ.

On February 4, 1942, Dietrich passed his thirty-sixth birthday quietly. He had little reason to celebrate. His brother-in-law Hans had just informed him that his mail was being read and his telephone tapped.

Aware that he could be arrested at any time, Dietrich wrote up a will, which he gave to Eberhard for safekeeping. He also set up a coding system that could be used to smuggle messages in and out of prison if necessary. The system relied on the hope that if Dietrich or other members of the family were arrested they would be able to swap books. It was decided that if a book arrived with the owner's name underlined on the flyleaf (a blank page at the end of a book), there was a message inside. The code consisted of spelling out words by placing a tiny pencil dot under a letter on every tenth page of the book, starting from the back. The dot was almost impossible to see unless a person was looking for it. Dietrich tried the technique several times and showed his parents and brothers and sisters how it worked. He hoped none of them would ever have to use the secret system.

Once Dietrich had his will and the secret coding system in place, he could do nothing more but continue his work as a pastor and a spy. He kept in constant touch with his students from the Finkenwalde seminary. The letters sent from the front lines from those serving in the military were grim. One wrote,

> For days at a stretch we cannot even wash our hands, but go from dead bodies to a meal and from there back to the rifle. . . . We often dream of being relieved, but we are now reduced to forty men instead of 150, still more we dream of Germany—I dream of the "calm and quiet life in all godliness and integrity." But we do not, any of us, know whether we shall be allowed to go home again.

Another student wrote,

> In mid-January, a unit of our detachment had to shoot fifty prisoners in one day because we were on the march and could not take them with us. In districts where there are partisans, women and children who are suspected of supplying partisans with provisions have to

be killed by shooting them in the back of the neck. . . . "Blessed are the merciful for they will receive mercy" [Matthew 5:7]. The contradictions are enormous, for many, no doubt, unbearably great.

Not a week went by without news that one of Dietrich's brilliant young students had been killed in the fighting. Sometimes Dietrich was almost relieved that they had been removed from such a hellish situation.

Small glimmers of hope kept Dietrich going. He was heartened by the Norwegian church's response after the takeover of their country by the Nazis. When the Nazi-backed Norwegian prime minister, Vidkun Quisling, decided to crack down hard on the church, all of the bishops and pastors in the country severed their ties with the government and the state church. The organizer of the church resistance in Norway, Bishop Eivind Berggrav, declared boldly to Norwegian pastors, "Take your wives and children along and travel the roads with a handcart. Hold a parish meeting every evening. I am sure that if Norway's thousand pastors set out that way, the men in Berlin will understand fast enough how foolish this whole business is." Shortly afterward, Bishop Berggrav was arrested, but his arrest only strengthened church resistance.

Naturally these upstart Norwegian clergymen disturbed the Nazis, who wanted to know who was leading the rebellion with the bishop in jail. Abwehr was given the task of finding out. As a result,

Dietrich and another member of the conspiracy, Count Helmuth von Moltke, were sent to Norway. The count was a year younger than Dietrich and came from a long line of distinguished military men. His father had been the head of Germany's armed forces at the beginning of World War I, and his great-uncle had been a famous field marshal in the Franco-Prussian war. The count was a dedicated Christian who led a group of conspirators called the Kreisau Circle.

Unlike Dietrich, those involved in the Kreisau Circle did not believe it was wise to kill Adolf Hitler. They argued that if Hitler were assassinated, he would be hailed as a martyr, and if they failed in the assassination attempt, thousands of resistance members would be hunted down and executed. Neither outcome was acceptable to the Kreisau Circle. Dietrich understood their point, but he felt it was worth the risk. Hitler had to go, and the sooner the better.

Dietrich and Helmuth became friends during their assignment in Norway. Because of his family's long and illustrious military history, the count was able to meet with many German officers commanding the occupation force in Norway, while Dietrich worked behind the scenes encouraging the Norwegian church leaders in their resistance.

The real purpose of Dietrich and Helmuth's visit to Norway was to try to save the life of Bishop Berggrav, who would almost certainly be tried and executed for his part in the resistance. The plan worked. Based on the information Dietrich and Helmuth reported to Abwehr, a short time later an order for Bishop Berggrav's release was sent to Norway from Berlin. Keeping the bishop in jail was only aggravating the resistance in Norway.

Upon his return from Norway, Dietrich learned that Bishop George Bell was visiting Sweden for three weeks. When Hans and Admiral Canaris learned this, they quickly organized a trip to Sweden for Dietrich, securing a courier pass for him through the Foreign Ministry. As soon as the paperwork was in order, Dietrich flew from Berlin to Stockholm, Sweden. He arrived in Stockholm on May 31, 1942, and learned that Bishop Bell was at the Nordic Ecumenical Institute in Sigtuna, to the north. Dietrich quickly made his way there, surprising the bishop when he appeared unannounced at the institute. Dietrich and Bishop Bell had not seen each other since 1939, just before Dietrich left for the United States. The two men enjoyed a warm reunion and talked for several hours, catching each other up on what they had been doing. Bishop Bell also reported that Dietrich's sister Sabine and her husband, Gerhard, were doing well. They were still in Oxford, and Gerhard was a helpful adviser to the bishop on matters related to Germany.

Dietrich then filled Bishop Bell in on what was happening with the conspiracy. He gave the bishop the names of current generals involved and new details on how they planned to assassinate Hitler and overthrow the Nazis. He also told him who would most likely lead a new German government after that. Again he put out feelers for the kind of peace terms the British government might be willing to negotiate.

Bishop Bell promised Dietrich he would do all in his power to get the information to the right people in the British government. However, he sounded a note of caution. The British had entered into an alliance with the Soviet Union. Given the carnage and death the Germans had wrought in Russia, British Prime Minister Winston Churchill was even less inclined to make any distinction between Nazis and other Germans, even those wanting to overthrow Hitler. Still, Bishop Bell hoped the specific information and names Dietrich had provided would help change some minds in the government when they saw that there was a real conspiracy with real and well-placed people behind it. Dietrich hoped that would be the case.

When he arrived back in Germany, Dietrich learned that Reinhard Heydrich, one of the architects of the Final Solution—the plan to exterminate the Jews in Europe—had been assassinated by two resistance fighters in Prague, Czechoslovakia. Learning that such an evil man had been done away with was encouraging to Dietrich, but the Nazi reprisals against the Czechs that followed were not. As usual, the Nazis were thorough, ordering the execution of hundreds of men, women, and children whom they believed came from the same town as the assassins. Dietrich hoped all the madness and killing would soon be over.

Chapter 16

Maria

A week after his return from Sweden, Dietrich sat in the dining room at Ruth von Kleist-Retzow's estate at Klein-Krössin in Pomerania, talking with Ruth and her eighteen-year-old granddaughter, Maria. Maria had just graduated from high school and was preparing for a year of national service. She explained to Dietrich that she hoped to be assigned to a hospital as a nursing assistant. Dietrich asked about her long-term plans, and Maria told him she would like to be a mathematician.

Dietrich was impressed by Maria's intelligence and confidence. He thought of the other times he'd met her—when she came to open meetings at the Finkenwalde seminary with her grandmother, when he baptized her older brother Max, and when he was

introduced to her parents, Hans and Ruth von Wedemeyer, who were both outstanding Christian leaders
in their community.

After lunch Dietrich and Maria took a stroll in
the garden. It was a warm summer day, and Ruth's
roses were in full bloom. Maria told Dietrich that
her father was now commanding an infantry battalion near Stalingrad in the Soviet Union and how he
hated the fact that he was fighting to keep a man as
evil as Adolf Hitler in power. Dietrich tried to comfort Maria. He knew just how nerve-racking it was to
have family members in the military.

Maria left early the next morning. As Dietrich
continued his writing, he found his mind wander-
ing back to the conversations he'd had with her. *She
really is quite extraordinary for such a young woman*, he
thought. After a refreshing week at Klein-Krössin,
Dietrich caught the train back to Munich.

His next assignment with Abwehr was to accompany Hans to Venice and Rome on official business. As Dietrich was being driven around Rome,
he couldn't help thinking of the wonderful times he
and Klaus had had there when they visited eighteen
years before. How different things were now.

Dietrich arrived back in Germany in mid-August
to learn that Maria and Max von Wedemeyer's father
had been killed in the fighting in the Soviet Union.
Dietrich wrote to the family, encouraging them to
remain strong in their faith. As soon as he could,
he visited Ruth at Klein-Krössin to pay his respects
on the death of her son-in-law. Dietrich noticed that

Ruth was having increasing difficulty reading as her eyesight began to fail. When Dietrich returned to Berlin to visit his parents, he arranged for Ruth to come to Berlin for eye surgery at the Franciscan Hospital.

Maria, who had not yet been assigned to a hospital as part of her national service, came along to assist her grandmother. Dietrich met her at the hospital several times and used the opportunity to talk with her about her father's death. Dietrich also told her about some of his work in the resistance. He knew she would be sympathetic, given her father's opposition to the Nazis, and because her uncle, Major General Henning von Tresckow, was heavily involved in the conspiracy to kill Hitler.

The following week Dietrich invited Maria to meet his family at a gathering in honor of one of his nephews going off to fight in the war. Even though she was much younger than he, Dietrich felt an attraction to Maria. As difficult as it was for him to believe, he knew he was in love with her.

Just two months after Maria's father's death, Maria's brother Max was killed in the war. Dietrich was deeply disturbed when he learned this and wrote to Maria offering his condolences. It was a setback for Dietrich's romantic plans, since Maria was now mourning the loss of both her father and her brother.

Strangely, as Dietrich wrestled with his feelings toward Maria, his close friend Eberhard confided that he also was in love with a young woman. The woman he had fallen in love with was someone Dietrich knew well—eighteen-year-old Renate

Schleicher, the daughter of his older sister Ursula and her husband, Rüdiger. Dietrich and Eberhard found themselves in quite a quandary. Maria's family was in disarray, and Ursula and Rüdiger thought Renate too young to marry.

Dietrich began writing to Maria, explaining how he felt. At first she was astonished but agreed to continue corresponding. Gradually, as they continued to write letters back and forth, she fell in love with Dietrich. On January 17, 1943, Maria wrote to Dietrich responding to his proposal in a previous letter. She said, "Today I can say yes to you from my entire, joyful heart." With that, Dietrich Bonhoeffer and Maria von Wedemeyer were officially engaged to be married.

The couple didn't set a marriage date. Because so many things were up in the air in Germany and in their lives, Dietrich did not want to make Maria his wife until things had settled down. In particular, two very different events were on the horizon, and the order in which they occurred could change everything. The first was Operation Flash, another attempt to assassinate Adolf Hitler. Operation Flash called for a bomb to be placed on Hitler's airplane while he visited German troops in Smolensk in the Soviet Union in March. If all went according to plan, the bomb would explode while Hitler was flying back to East Prussia, killing him and all aboard the plane.

The second event was Dietrich's probable arrest. Hans had told Dietrich that he was now certain the Gestapo was tailing them. Hans explained he believed the Gestapo had uncovered the money trail he had used to acquire the foreign currency the Swiss government demanded before allowing the fourteen Jews of Operation 7 to flee to freedom. And since Dietrich had been involved in Operation 7, the Gestapo was also on his trail. At some stage, Hans was certain, they would both be arrested. The question looming over Dietrich was, which would happen first, his arrest or Hitler's death?

Tension mounted as Operation Flash grew near. Hans had recruited Eberhard into Abwehr to keep him from being drafted into the army, and on the evening of March 12, 1943, he had Eberhard drive him to the railway station. The package Hans carried on the night train east contained the bomb to be used to kill Hitler.

Hans was to take the bomb to Smolensk, where he would hand it over to Maria's uncle, Major General Henning von Tresckow, and his aide, Fabian von Schlabrendorff, who happened to be married to Maria's cousin. It was the job of these two to get the bomb onto the airplane Hitler would be flying in and then detonate the chemical fuse before the plane took off. If all went as planned, the bomb would explode approximately thirty minutes later, just as Adolf Hitler was flying over Minsk.

On March 13, Dietrich and the other conspirators waited nervously for news that the plane had exploded, but none came. Instead, Hitler's plane landed safely in East Prussia. Now they were sick with worry. Had the bomb been found? With incredible coolness, Major General von Tresckow called to find out what had happened to the "package." He learned that the bomb hadn't been discovered on the airplane but had failed to detonate during the flight. It was a relief to all in the conspiracy that Hitler didn't realize how close he had come to dying. They would try again.

The next assassination attempt occurred eight days later and was more direct. It was a suicide mission in which a Major Rudolf-Christoph von Gersdorff would meet Adolf Hitler, Heinrich Himmler, and Hermann Göring at the Heroes' Memorial Day ceremony in Berlin. The major would carry two bombs in his overcoat and detonate them when he was close to all three Nazi leaders. This time the fuses would detonate in ten minutes.

While the assassination attempt was under way, Dietrich, Rüdiger Schleicher, and Hans were all assembled at the Schleicher home. They were rehearsing a musical performance for Dietrich's father's seventy-fifth birthday in ten days. As they practiced, they glanced nervously at each other. Dietrich knew what the others were thinking. At any moment now the führer and two of his worst henchmen would be dead. The Third Reich would at last be over.

The minutes ticked by. Dietrich played piano while Rüdiger accompanied on the violin and Hans sang. With each note he sounded on the piano, Dietrich waited anxiously for the phone to ring, but no call came. By the end of the rehearsal, it was clear that something had gone wrong again. Hitler appeared to have more lives than a cat.

Later Dietrich learned that Hitler had stayed at the ceremony for only a few minutes, even though he was scheduled to be there for a half hour. There was not enough time to activate the bomb. As the war progressed, Hitler had become deliberately more unpredictable about his movements.

In the meantime, the Bonhoeffer clan gathered for Karl Bonhoeffer's seventy-fifth birthday. Everyone was there except Sabine, Gerhard, and their two girls. Eberhard and Dietrich's niece Renate were particularly happy. Renate's parents, Ursula and Rüdiger, had granted permission for the two to marry the following month.

For one happy day, the Bonhoeffer family tried to forget about the war. There was food, wine, music, and poetry, just as there had been at so many other wonderful family gatherings. What no one knew was that this would be the last time they were all together.

Chapter 17

Cell 92

At noon on April 5, 1943, Dietrich was at his parents' house and decided to call the Dohnanyis. He dialed the number and waited for Christine to pick up the phone. Instead a clipped male voice answered. Dietrich knew it wasn't Hans's voice and immediately put down the receiver. He took a deep breath. *So the time has come,* he thought. *I will be next.* He was sure that the voice on the phone belonged to a Gestapo agent and that the Dohnanyis' house was being searched. Not wanting to alarm his parents, Dietrich calmly walked next door to where Ursula and Rüdiger lived. Eberhard was visiting his future in-laws at the time.

Dietrich explained the situation to the three of them, and then Ursula prepared a meal for them all.

Dietrich heartily ate the food put in front of him, not knowing when he might eat this well again. As they sat around the table, they discussed Hitler's first big defeat. It had happened just two months before in Stalingrad. The German army had fought through the winter for control of the city, but weak, hungry, and without hope of reinforcements, Field Marshal Friedrich Paulus had surrendered to the Soviets. It was the first time Hitler had acknowledged a defeat to the German people. And in January, the Americans had flown a bombing raid over Wilhelmshaven, a coastal town in northern Germany. Everyone in the room hoped that the war would end soon.

Dietrich stayed at the Schleichers' home until just after four in the afternoon, when his father came to tell him two men were waiting for him back at the house. Dietrich hugged Ursula, shook hands with Rüdiger and Eberhard, and walked quietly next door with his father. The two men were standing in the hallway. Dietrich immediately recognized one of them, Colonel Manfred Roeder, a senior military prosecutor. He greeted the prosecutor cordially, and the two men escorted him upstairs to his room. Dietrich was told to stand still while the men proceeded to tear his room apart. They pulled out drawers and turned them upside down and poked at the ceiling panels. Dietrich grabbed his Bible as the men loaded papers into a large cardboard box. Finally the two men took Dietrich by the arm and escorted him downstairs and out the front door of the house to a waiting black Mercedes-Benz. Dietrich was pushed into the back seat. He gripped his Bible and gazed back at the house. His parents stood silently in front of the gate.

The Mercedes sped north through the streets of Berlin. There was little traffic, as gasoline was now severely rationed for everyone except Nazis on government business. Soon Dietrich was led into Tegel Military Prison with its whitewashed walls and red tiled roof.

Night was falling by the time Dietrich was escorted through the doors and shoved into a receiving cell. A guard took his Bible and threw a blanket at him before the cell door clanged shut. Dietrich recoiled at the foul-smelling blanket, which he couldn't even bear to cover himself with. He spent a long night curled up on a hard cot, trying to block out the sound of other prisoners weeping and groaning. Early the next morning a guard opened the door and threw a piece of bread onto the floor. Dietrich bent down and picked it up.

Later Dietrich was taken up to the fourth floor and locked in a cell. The room was seven feet wide by ten feet long and held a wooden bed, a stool, a bucket, and a bench along the wall. Above the bench a previous prisoner had scratched the words, "In a hundred years it will all be over." Dietrich soon learned from the guards that it would probably be over for him long before that. The fourth floor was where prisoners condemned to death were housed. About twenty men each week were marched from their cells, never to return, presumably executed. The cells they left behind were never empty for more than an hour as more men were marched upstairs to take their place. The noise of prisoners wailing and cursing as they awaited their fate kept Dietrich awake at night.

On Dietrich's third day of incarceration in Tegel, a guard returned his Bible. By now Dietrich had adjusted to the shock of being arrested and devised a plan to keep himself focused on God and others. He began each day with Bible reading, hymn singing, meditation, Scripture memorization, and physical exercises.

Most times Dietrich stayed calm and focused, but a week into his imprisonment he was handcuffed and driven into the heart of Berlin to be interrogated. He knew the interrogations with Colonel Roeder would be his biggest challenge. Dietrich didn't want to draw attention to anyone else or divulge any information that would endanger his friends. Being up against a brilliant man like Roeder, who was intent on getting to the bottom of what had been going on in Abwehr, was nerve-racking. Dietrich was unsure of what accusations had been made against him and what Roeder knew. This made it difficult for Dietrich to gauge what to say. Dietrich remembered Hans's instruction to plead ignorance and shift the responsibility to Hans as much as possible. Hans had explained that he was familiar with the legal process and questioning and would do a better job of deflecting questions. Dietrich tried hard to follow the advice, though it was difficult, knowing that he was probably making life harder for his brother-in-law. Thankfully, after several interrogation sessions, Colonel Roeder seemed to accept that Dietrich was a pastor with limited knowledge of the inner workings of Abwehr.

Dietrich was allowed to write a single, one-page letter every ten days. He wrote to his parents first. He couldn't imagine the burden his arrest had placed on them. He wrote, "I am now learning daily how good my life with you has always been, and besides, I now have to practice myself what I have told others in my sermons and books."

Dietrich knew that the letters he sent and those he received were censored, but the first letter he received from his parents still contained plenty of information—none of it hopeful. On the day Dietrich was arrested, Hans and Christine von Dohnanyi, along with Joseph Müller, an operative from Abwehr's Munich office, and his wife had also been arrested. The two men were taken to a military prison for ranking officers, while their wives went to a women's prison. None of them were allowed visitors, and Dietrich's parents were concerned about them all.

Not long after receiving the letter from his parents, Dietrich was transferred to cell 92 on the third floor of Tegel Prison. From the cell's window Dietrich could see out over the prison yard and beyond to a pine forest. It reminded him of his childhood, playing in the forest in the Harz Mountains. How far away that time seemed from his damp, smelly cell.

Dietrich soon began making friends with his guards. Most knew he was a pastor, and slowly they began confiding in him. Some wanted prayer, others advice. Dietrich realized many of the guards were trapped in their roles. They despised Hitler as much as he did, but if they spoke out or refused to do their duty, they would end up on the inside of a cell instead of guarding the cells from the outside. Dietrich felt compassion for their plight and prayed for the guards regularly.

Even with his strict, self-imposed discipline, there were times when the days dragged and Dietrich wondered how his family and Maria were doing. He was relieved when a letter from Maria arrived, explaining that she had moved to Berlin. Dietrich's parents had invited her to stay with them. Karl Bonhoeffer had even secured the necessary paperwork so that Maria could be his secretary. Even at seventy-five years of age he still saw a few patients at home. It was a good solution, and Dietrich hoped that Maria would somehow gain permission to visit him in prison.

Another letter from his parents told Dietrich that his sister Christine had been released from prison but was now quite ill. Dietrich added Christine's condition to his prayer list.

Dietrich was finally allowed a visit from his parents. It disturbed him to see how much they had aged. His father looked frail. Dietrich tried to assure his father that he was being treated well, but his mother asked specific questions about his circumstances, and he did not lie. When she heard Dietrich's answers, she became indignant that her son was not allowed out of his cell to exercise and that he hadn't been able to receive any of the food parcels she had sent.

A week later, Dietrich's situation at Tegel Prison improved dramatically. Captain Maetz, the prison commandant, unlocked Dietrich's cell door and invited him outside for a walk in the prison yard. The sun on his back and a breeze in his face felt wonderful to Dietrich. As they walked together, Captain Maetz told Dietrich how surprised they had all been to learn that he was related to General Paul von Hase, the city commander of Berlin, including Tegel Prison. The captain apologized for any ill treatment Dietrich had endured and assured him he would now receive any parcels sent to him. Dietrich later learned that a well-placed phone call from his mother to her first cousin, Paul von Hase, had led to Captain Maetz's being alerted to the relationship between Dietrich, his prisoner, and the city commander, his boss.

On June 24, 1943, Dietrich was escorted down to the visitors' area. He stood waiting. When the door opened, Maria was standing in front of him. Dietrich was stunned to see his fiancée. He wanted to talk to her about deep issues, but as always, the guards were nearby, and they contented themselves with talk about their families and making plans for their wedding. Maria was able to give Dietrich a book he'd asked for. When he got back to his cell, he realized his name on the flyleaf in the back of the book was underlined—the book contained a message in the code the family had agreed upon before any family members had been arrested. He quickly looked for the dot under a letter on every tenth page going backward. From the message in that book and many other books that followed, Dietrich was able to learn what Hans was being interrogated about so that he could coordinate his story with that of his brother-in-law.

After Maria's visit, Dietrich was allowed more visitors and for longer periods. He never knew when he would get a visitor or how long he would be able to talk, but it felt wonderful to have contact with the outside world.

Within the prison, Dietrich befriended three guards in particular. All three hated the Third Reich and promised to do anything they could to help Dietrich. They supplied him with fresh writing paper and pens and smuggled letters in and out of the prison for him. This brightened Dietrich's life considerably, and he started writing a theology book that was smuggled out chapter by chapter to Eberhard Bethge. One of the guards also smuggled out a wedding sermon for Eberhard and Renate's wedding. Dietrich felt wistful the day of their wedding; he'd been asked to be Eberhard's best man.

The friendly guards continued to watch over Dietrich, allowing him to visit the infirmary to pray with the patients. Dietrich always focused on their practical as well as their spiritual needs. He also used his own money to hire lawyers for several of the prisoners who had suffered from shell shock while fighting on the front lines and had walked away from their posts, making them deserters. This was a crime punishable by death, but Dietrich hoped that with good representation the men could prove they were unaware of their actions at the time.

Dietrich loved his work in the infirmar~~y~~ came with an added bonus—he was able to the radio while there. What bliss it was to listen to broadcasts of concerts. The sound of beautiful music lifted his spirits. Sometimes, when only Dietrich's friendly guards were around, the guards even turned the radio dial to listen to news from the BBC in London.

In July 1943, Dietrich was finally charged with "subversion of the armed forces." A date was set for his trial, but the trial was postponed and another date set. This happened over and over until Dietrich wondered whether there would ever be a trial. In the meantime, Dietrich heard snippets of news about what was happening on the outside. That month the Allies had bombed Rome and Hamburg. Dietrich later learned that the Italians had surrendered to the Allies in early September, though German troops still occupied Rome and northern Italy.

On the night of November 26, Dietrich went from hearing about Allied air raids to experiencing one. Four days before, the Allies had launched a series of air bombings over Berlin. But on the night of the twenty-sixth, the Borsig locomotive factory, right next to Tegel Prison, was a target of the Allied bombing. The prison shook as exploding bombs crashed nearby.

The next morning Dietrich learned from a guard that the bombing had been severe. As a result, fires were burning all over the city, and around 2,000 Berliners had been killed and another 175,000 left homeless. The Kaiser Wilhelm Memorial Church, where Dietrich had preached on several occasions, was badly damaged, along with the zoo and Charlottenburg Palace. Dietrich waited anxiously for a letter from his parents. Thankfully everyone in the Bonhoeffer household was safe.

As Christmas 1943 approached, the official prison pastor asked Dietrich to write prayers for the prisoners to recite. Dietrich was glad to do so, and the prayers were distributed throughout Tegel. For Dietrich, it was a lonely Christmas being locked up away from his family.

When 1944 began, Dietrich wondered what the year ahead would hold. Would the war be over soon? Would he get his trial and a chance at freedom? By the end of January, he received one piece of good news: Colonel Manfred Roeder had been dismissed as the chief prosecutor for Dietrich's case, and a new prosecutor had been assigned in his place. Dietrich hoped this would hurry along the legal process. Meanwhile, the area around Tegel Prison was now being repeatedly bombed in Allied bombing raids.

February, though, brought bad news: Admiral Canaris had been suspended, and Abwehr had been integrated into the Office for National Security. As head of Abwehr, Admiral Canaris had done all he could to watch out for Dietrich and Hans in prison. That protection no longer existed.

Eberhard visited, and Sergeant Linke, one of the three guards helpful to Dietrich, allowed the two men to visit each other without anyone monitoring their conversation. Dietrich felt relief in being able to talk freely to his best friend. Eberhard announced that he'd been drafted into the army and was being sent to serve on the Italian Front. In addition, his wife Renate, Dietrich's niece, was pregnant. Eberhard also told Dietrich that Hans was not doing well. Hans had suffered a stroke and was partially blind and losing hope. Dietrich took off his wire-rimmed glasses and rubbed his forehead at the discouraging news.

Life continued on day after day in Tegel. Dietrich kept up his self-imposed activity schedule and read a number of books. He knew he could push for his case to be reassessed, but contacts outside the prison urged him to wait. Another assassination attempt on Hitler's life was being planned for July 20, 1944. This attempt involved Count von Stauffenberg's leaving a bomb in a briefcase at field headquarters in Rastenburg, East Prussia, while Hitler was visiting.

On July 20, Dietrich listened intently to the infirmary radio, waiting for news of Hitler's death. The BBC interrupted its broadcast with a news flash, but it was not the news Dietrich hoped to hear. The BBC reported that an assassination attempt had been made on the führer's life but that Hitler had escaped with only minor injuries, while a stenographer and three officers had been killed. Dietrich could hardly believe it. Once again Adolf Hitler had cheated death.

Reprisals for the failed assassination attempt were swift and thorough. Within days about two hundred men and women suspected of playing a role in the plot were rounded up, tortured, and killed. Among the suspects was Dietrich's mother's cousin, General Paul von Hase.

Two months later, Dietrich heard more devastating news. On September 22, the Nazis discovered Hans von Dohnanyi's "Chronicle of Shame." After his arrest Hans had sent instructions via his wife, Christine, to destroy the documents. The instructions weren't followed, however, and the "Chronicle of Shame" was left in an Abwehr safe in the town of Zossen, on the outskirts of Berlin, where the Nazis discovered it. Now Hitler could read the dossier for himself. Dietrich knew that it showed that he, Admiral Canaris, General Hans Oster, Hans von Dohnanyi, and a number of others were involved in an earlier conspiracy to kill Hitler. It was now only a matter of time before these men were killed for their role in the plot.

Knowing this, by early October, Dietrich's family had come up with a plan to get Dietrich out of jail. One of the friendly guards would bring civilian clothes into the prison for Dietrich, who would put them on and walk out of Tegel dressed as a prison gardener. Dietrich was ready to follow their plan, until he learned of the arrests of his brother Klaus, his brother-in-law Rüdiger, and his friend Eberhard on October 4. The men had all been arrested for their involvement in the wider conspiracy to assassinate Hitler and overthrow the Nazis. Dietrich immediately abandoned his escape plan for fear that retribution might fall on Maria and the rest of his family. Now all he could do was wait.

Four days later, on October 8, 1944, Dietrich was transferred from Tegel Military Prison to the Gestapo prison on Prinz-Albrecht-Strasse. This was not a good sign.

Chapter 18

Our Victory Is Certain

Within a day of arriving at the Gestapo prison in the basement of the Reich Main Security Office, Dietrich realized the prison held some advantages. His cell was smaller than the previous one. Because it had barely room for a folding bed and a stool, Dietrich had to use the communal bathroom at the end of the cellblock. This brought him into contact with other prisoners. Even though the prisoners were not supposed to talk to each other, Dietrich discovered that the noise of running water covered their whispered conversations. Because of this, everyone was eager to take a shower, even though the water was cold.

No outside exercise was allowed, but the prisoners were all hustled out of their cells during the frequent air raids and taken down a corridor to a bunker. The Gestapo still thought there was important information to extract from its prisoners and didn't want them killed in an air raid. Everyone took advantage of the chaos of getting to the bunker to exchange greetings and information with other prisoners they knew. Dietrich was not surprised to recognize Admiral Canaris and General Oster during one air raid. Both men looked ill and gaunt.

Between air raids Dietrich continued to write, though sometimes he ran short of paper. He was able to have some visitors and receive food and book parcels, though not as frequently as at Tegel.

Dietrich entered 1945 with a sense of urgency. His only hope, and that of his brother and brothers-in-law, was for the Allies to smash the Nazis soon. Not only were the Allies now bombing Germany at will from the air, but the Soviet army was also sweeping in from the east, and British, French, and American troops were pushing in from the west. It was only a matter of time before Germany was defeated.

As Dietrich was being herded to the bomb shelter at the beginning of February, he looked into one cell and saw his brother-in-law Hans lying on a stretcher. In the mayhem of prisoners rushing toward the bunker, Dietrich slipped into Hans's cell and talked to him briefly. Hans told him he'd been transferred to the Gestapo prison the day before. Dietrich could see that he was in terrible shape physically from sickness, torture, and neglect. Dietrich could spend only a few moments with Hans before he had to rejoin the other prisoners. Soon afterward he learned that Hans had been moved to a military hospital.

On February 3, 1945, almost a thousand US Air Force B-17 bombers attacked Berlin. For two hours Dietrich listened from the prison bomb shelter as wave after wave of airplanes flew overhead. At times the exploding bombs shook the earth so much that Dietrich thought the roof would cave in. But the bomb shelter held together. The Reich Main Security Office did not fare so well. It was almost completely destroyed by the bombing. The Gestapo prison in the basement was still intact, but it was obvious to Dietrich and the other prisoners that they couldn't be housed there much longer.

The day after the bombing attack, Dietrich had his thirty-ninth birthday. He said special prayers for his sister Sabine and her family; he was glad they were safe in England. He also prayed for his aging parents, knowing they would spend the day thinking about him and Sabine. He hoped that perhaps next year he and his twin sister could spend their birthday together again. Dietrich was sure his parents and Maria would try to get a birthday parcel to him, and he was concerned about the dangers they would face walking about the bombed-out city. Dietrich was right. On the morning of February 7, he received a birthday parcel.

Around noon that day, a commotion started outside Dietrich's cell. Soon the cell door swung open, and Dietrich was ordered to gather up his things and stand outside his cell in the corridor. Dietrich was then marched outside the prison and told to wait with twenty other men. It was the first time he had seen daylight in the four months since arriving at the Gestapo prison. Dietrich recognized some of the men he was waiting with: General von Falkenhausen, who had been the governor of Belgium when Germany occupied the country during World War I; Kurt von Schuschnigg, the former chancellor of Austria; Hjalmar Schacht, the former head of the Reichsbank; Admiral Canaris, General Hans Oster, Judge Karl Sack, and Joseph Müller, who had worked out of the Munich office of Abwehr; and various other military officers.

Finally two battered vans pulled up to transport the prisoners. For some reason Dietrich and Joseph Müller were handcuffed before being ordered into one of the vans. The engine revved and the vans were off. As they drove through the streets of Berlin, Dietrich was shocked by what he saw. The bombs had leveled buildings, and in some cases, whole blocks. The roads were pockmarked, and there didn't seem to be any direction you could turn and not see damage. A haze of smoke from the smoldering hulks of bombed and burned-out buildings hung in the air.

From Berlin the vans headed in a southwesterly direction through the countryside. So many things seemed normal: sunshine, green grass in the fields, and open blue sky above. Yet Dietrich dreaded reaching their destination—Buchenwald Concentration Camp, 160 miles away. Even with all he knew, Dietrich was appalled by what he saw when the vans reached Buchenwald. Living skeletons with dark sunken eyes, some of them children as young as three, stared blankly at the new arrivals.

By nightfall the prisoners were incarcerated in a dark, damp prison in the basement of a large building outside the main Buchenwald compound. The basement was divided into cells. Dietrich's handcuffs were taken off, and he was given the first food he'd had all day—a piece of bread and lard. He was assigned to Cell 1, next to the washroom. He was alone in the cell. Cell 2 housed Dr. Hermann Pünder, a Catholic politician. In the morning Dietrich struck up a conversation with him, and the two of them spent many hours talking about how Protestants and Catholics could work together after the war.

No one was allowed outside the basement prison to exercise. Instead the men were all let out of their cells together and allowed to walk up and down the corridor in a long line. This was comforting to Dietrich, who was able to smile and greet old friends and acquaintances and meet some of the new prisoners.

After Dietrich had been underground for two weeks, General Friedrich von Rabenau joined him as his cellmate. Sixty-year-old General von Rabenau was a Berliner who had been Chief of the Army Archives before earning a degree in theology at the University of Berlin. He had been arrested after the last attempt to assassinate Hitler. Friedrich was a dedicated Christian, and Dietrich was delighted to have him as a cellmate. The two of them had many things in common.

Since Cell 1 was next to the bathroom, Dietrich and the general could time their requests to be escorted there to coincide with the visits of other prisoners. As soon as possible, Friedrich arranged to introduce Dietrich to Payne Best, an English intelligence officer captured by the Nazis in Holland at the end of 1939. Payne had been placed at several different concentration camps since then. He and Friedrich and several others had just been transferred to Buchenwald.

Payne was a larger-than-life character, and Dietrich enjoyed speaking with him in English. Payne gave Dietrich a chess set, and Dietrich and Friedrich passed the hours together in their cell playing chess.

For seven weeks there was little news from above ground. However, on Easter Sunday, April 1, 1945, Dietrich felt his cell shaking. It could mean only one thing—the Allies were bombing close by. Dietrich's hopes rose. Perhaps the war was nearly over.

Two days later Dietrich and fifteen other prisoners (both men and women) were marched upstairs and ordered into the back of a large, enclosed truck. Dietrich climbed into the back and squeezed his body around a large pile of split wood. As the truck rolled away from Buchenwald, he realized it had been adapted to run off power provided by a generator, which was in turn powered by a small furnace that burned wood, hence the wood in the back. It was already dark when they set out, making it difficult to get a bearing on where they were headed. Someone estimated they were traveling at about twenty miles an hour. At dawn a prisoner caught a glimpse of a village he recognized and yelled back that they were headed southeast. Dietrich's heart sank. It could only mean they were headed for Flossenbürg Concentration Camp.

The truck lurched along, stopping every hour so the guards could refuel the furnace and clean the flue. Each time wood was loaded into the furnace, the men and women in back had just a little more room.

Early on Wednesday afternoon the truck reached Weiden, the turnoff to Flossenbürg. The truck halted, and a conversation ensued between their guard and another man. In the course of the conversation Dietrich heard the other man say, "Drive on, we can't take you . . . too full." With that, the truck moved on. Dietrich and the other prisoners breathed a deep sigh of relief. They would not be going to Flossenbürg after all.

After about two hours of driving, the truck stopped outside a Bavarian farm and everyone was allowed out. The farmer's wife welcomed the group and offered them milk and dark rye bread. It was the best food Dietrich had eaten in months, and he was grateful for it.

The truck continued its journey southward, and the guards, who seemed to Dietrich to be a little confused about their destination, became friendlier after the stop at the farm. They left the cover over the window in the truck's back door open so the prisoners could see blue sky. The sky looked wonderful to Dietrich after so long in a dark basement cell. At dusk they stopped in Regensburg. Dietrich could hear the guards negotiating with various officials, but no one had room for them or their prisoners. Eventually a deal was struck. The prisoners could stay in five cells in the basement of the jail attached to the courthouse. The prisoners were crammed five to a cell, but they were treated well. That night Dietrich enjoyed a good night's sleep on a mattress of straw.

The following morning, when the cell doors opened so the prisoners could wash, a huge surprise awaited them. The corridor was filled with men, women, and children, all relatives of the people who had been killed for their part in the von Stauffenberg assassination attempt on Hitler. They were being held in the cells on the first and second floors of the prison. Dietrich recognized some of the men from the Gestapo prison on Prinz-Albrecht-Strasse and was able to pass information to them about their relatives' last words and deeds.

Despite the somber topic, there were many joyful reunions. The guards found it difficult to control the prisoners and in the end gave up, allowing the prisoners to spend much of the day together. At five in the afternoon, the Buchenwald guards showed up and ordered Dietrich and the other Buchenwald prisoners back into the truck. This time Dietrich climbed aboard with a light heart. How wonderful it was to reunite with the families of old friends and acquaintances.

Not far outside of Regensburg, the truck broke an axle. Everyone spent a cold night waiting for help to

arrive. At eleven the next morning, a bus with pad-
ded seats arrived to pick up the prisoners. Dietrich
climbed aboard, sank into a seat, and stared out the
plate-glass window. It felt so civilized.

As the bus rumbled through the countryside, Dietrich could see how much damage the Allied bombing had caused. Craters pockmarked the earth, and
burned-out cars littered the side of the road. At one
in the afternoon, the bus pulled up outside a school
in the village of Schönberg. The school was now a
makeshift prison, and Dietrich and the others were
marched to the first floor, into a classroom being used
as a dormitory. What they encountered seemed like
a dream to Dietrich—feather beds, bright-colored
bedspreads, and large windows overlooking a beautiful valley. Food was scarce, but a meal of potatoes
and coffee was provided. Once again Dietrich slept
soundly.

The following day, Saturday, was beautiful, and
the prisoners relaxed at Schönberg. Payne Best produced a razor, and all the men shaved and washed.
More family members of men involved in the resistance were housed in the makeshift prison, and once
again Dietrich was able to make acquaintances and
pass on information.

April 8 was the first Sunday after Easter—Qua-
simodo Sunday—and the prisoners asked Dietrich to
lead them in a church service. Dietrich chose 1 Peter
1:3 as his text: "Blessed be the God and Father of our
Lord Jesus Christ! By His great mercy we have been
born anew to a living hope through the resurrection

of Jesus Christ from the dead." Just as Dietrich finished his short sermon, the door burst open and two men in civilian clothes pointed to him. "Prisoner Bonhoeffer, get ready to come with us," one of the men snapped.

Everyone in the room stood silently as Dietrich gathered his few belongings. He had a moment to say his farewells. On his way out, Dietrich stopped beside the Englishman Payne Best and said, "Please tell Bishop Bell from me, this is the end, but also the beginning. Like him, I believe in the principle of our Universal Christian Brotherhood, which rises above all national interests, and that our victory is certain." Then he turned and left with the two men.

Outside, Dietrich was loaded into the back of a van that sped off. Before long he was certain they were headed toward Flossenbürg. Sure enough, after several hours of driving on clogged roads, the van pulled into Flossenbürg Concentration Camp.

Dietrich was immediately taken to an area set up as a courtroom. He learned that earlier that day Admiral Wilhelm Canaris, General Hans Oster, Judge Karl Sack, and two other men from Abwehr had been tried for treason. Now, late on Sunday night, it was Dietrich's turn. The proceedings were quick and one-sided, after which Dietrich was taken to a solitary cell. He knew his only hope of living was for the Allies to arrive during the night. They did not.

At dawn the next day, Monday, April 9, 1945, two years and four days after his arrest, Dietrich Bonhoeffer was marched from his cell for the last time.

He joined the five other men as the guilty verdict was read and their death sentence handed down. Dietrich knelt in prayer. Then, like the others, he was told to strip naked and step outside. It was a damp, foggy morning. The gallows awaited. Dietrich bowed his head, said a brief prayer, and climbed the steps to the gallows. His death was mercifully fast. Afterward his body was burned, along with his few possessions.

> Who can comprehend how those whom God takes so early are chosen? Does not the early death of young Christians always appear to us as if God were plundering his own best instruments in a time in which they are most needed? Yet the Lord makes no mistakes. Might God need our brothers for some hidden service on our behalf in the heavenly world? We should put an end to our human thoughts, which always wish to know more than they can, and cling to that which is certain. Whomever God calls home is someone God has loved. "For their souls were pleasing to the Lord, therefore he took them quickly from the midst of wickedness" (Wisdom of Solomon 4).

> —Dietrich Bonhoeffer
> Letter to the Confessing Churches, August 1941

———————————————————————

Two weeks after Dietrich Bonhoeffer was hanged at Flossenbürg, American troops liberated the concentration camp on April 23, 1945. Payne Best survived his capture and was able to recount the events of Dietrich Bonhoeffer's last week.

At a meeting on Thursday, April 5, Adolf Hitler had declared that Bonhoeffer and Hans von Dohnanyi were not to survive, and an order was issued for their execution.

On the morning of Friday, April 6, a sick and frail Dohnanyi was transferred from the hospital in Berlin to Sachsenhausen Concentration Camp. On the morning of Monday, April 9, as Dietrich was being executed at Flossenbürg, Dohnanyi was court-martialed and executed at Sachsenhausen.

Klaus Bonhoeffer and Rüdiger Schleicher had been sentenced to death on February 2, 1945. On the night of April 22, they were both taken from their cells at the Gestapo prison on Lehrter Strasse in Berlin and shot. Eight days later, on April 30, Adolf Hitler committed suicide.

On May 8, the surrender of Germany to the Allies d. The war in Europe was over. Diet- nd, Eberhard Bethge, was still awaiting olvement in the resistance when Soviet d the prison where he was being held.

Bethge, Eberhard. *Costly Grace: An Illustrated Introduction to Dietrich Bonhoeffer.* New York: Harper & Row, 1979.

Bethge, Eberhard. *Dietrich Bonhoeffer: A Biography.* Minneapolis: Fortress Press, 2000.

Bethge, Renate, and Christian Gremmels, ed. *Dietrich Bonhoeffer: A Life in Pictures.* Minneapolis: Fortress Press, 2006.

Metaxas, Eric. *Bonhoeffer: Pastor, Martyr, Prophet, Spy.* Nashville: Thomas Nelson, 2010.

Schlingensiepen, Ferdinand. *Dietrich Bonhoeffer 1906–1945: Martyr, Thinker, Man of Resistance.* New York: T & T Clark, 2010.